AGRI-DAGH
MOUNT ARARAT

The Painful Mountain

AGRI-DAGH
MOUNT ARARAT

The Painful Mountain

by Dr. Don Shockey

with a presentation of evidence
for the scientific case for creation, entitled
A Look at Genesis and Science
by
Dr. Walter Brown

TEACH Services, Inc.
PUBLISHING
www.TEACHServices.com • (800) 367-1844

World rights reserved. This book or any portion thereof may not be copied or reproduced in any form or manner whatever, except as provided by law, without the written permission of the publisher, except by a reviewer who may quote brief passages in a review.

The author assumes full responsibility for the accuracy of all facts and quotations as cited in this book. The opinions expressed in this book are the author's personal views and interpretations, and do not necessarily reflect those of the publisher.

This book is provided with the understanding that the publisher is not engaged in giving spiritual, legal, medical, or other professional advice. If authoritative advice is needed, the reader should seek the counsel of a competent professional.

Copyright © 2018 TEACH Services, Inc.
ISBN-13: 978-1-57258-412-9 (Paperback)
Library of Congress Control Number: 2006920052

Facsimile Reproduction

As this book played a formative role in the development of Christian thought and the publisher feels that this book, with its candor and depth, still holds significance for the church today. Therefore the publisher has chosen to reproduce this historical classic from an original copy. Frequent variations in the quality of the print are unavoidable due to the condition of the original. Thus the print may look darker or lighter or appear to be missing detail, more in some places than in others.

To my family: My wife Carita and my daughters
D'Anne, Deborah, Delaine and Kendra,
who have helped me in so many ways
in my search for the truth.

"And they went in unto Noah into the ark, two and two of all flesh, wherein is the breath of life." "And they that went in, went in male and female of all flesh, as God had commanded him: **and the Lord shut him in."**

—Genesis 7:15-16

Contents

Preface ix

Photograph Credits xi

Part 1—The Ed Davis Story 1
Chapter 1, The First American to View Noah's Ark, 3. Chapter 2, Questions and Answers, 7. Chapter 3, Follow-Up Interviews, 17. Chapter 4, Description of the Ark, 22. Chapter 5, Fragmented Section of the Ark, 24. Chapter 6, Noah's Food and Fuel Supply, 26. Chapter 7, Verification, 28. Chapter 8, Weather Conditions, 30. Chapter 9, Ed Behling's Story, 35. Chapter 10, Can the Information Be Trusted?, 36. Chapter 11, In Conclusion, 39. Chapter 12, Synopsis of Ed Davis's Story, 42. Chapter 13, Some Personal History of Ed Davis, 44. Chapter 14, The Missing Russian Photographs of Noah's Ark, 45.

Suggested Reading 48

Photographs 51

Part 2—A Look at Genesis and Science by Dr. Walter Brown 89
Reference List, 112. About the Author, 144.

The "Deans" of All Ark Researchers, Eryl and Violet Cummings 145

Special Tribute to an Eminent Archaeologist and Ark Researcher, Dr. Howard Davis 146

F.I.B.E.R. 147

Preface

What you are about to read happened in the summer of 1943. Ed Davis, a sergeant in the American Army stationed in Hamadan, Iran, was allowed to accompany a band of Kurdish guardians of mankind's history to a hidden canyon high on the northeast slopes of Mount Ararat, where he viewed one of the greatest Biblical and archaeological treasures of all time—the Ark of Noah. His eye-witness account is being shared with the world for the first time. Ed Davis has given us new information, new insights into the Ark's shape, condition, construction and location, and a description of artifacts used by Noah and his family removed from the interior superstructure, as well as new understanding of why the Ark has remained so well hidden from searchers throughout the years. The importance of this new evidence provides yet additional testimony concerning the Biblical truth of the Flood. Why hasn't this story been shared before? The answer will appear as the story unfolds.

What subjects other than Noah's Ark and the Flood have been debated, argued, discussed, pondered, analyzed, rejected or accepted more often during the last two hundred years? Very few. Everyone has an opinion on the subject. Each is quick to respond from one of five different and opposing perspectives. The basis of one's belief is dictated by: (1) a Biblical or religious background; (2) a scientific-evolutionary platform; (3) a common-sense approach; (4) an "it doesn't really matter one way or the other attitude"; (5) a combination of parts or all of the above.

Why is it important anyway? If one accepts the scientific theory of evolution originated by Charles Darwin as a standard textbook formula and throws in a little uniformitarian geology which suggests "the present is a key to the past," and mixes this with some archaeology and the concept of fossil primates slowly becoming modern man, then problems and questions immediately arise as to the authenticity and reliability of the Genesis account of the Flood. Any other explanation of man's existence on this planet earth other than that which is evidenced by geological records, paleontology, archaeology, genetics and selective survival can be neither logical nor valid. To many in this group, the account of all living fauna being destroyed by a world-wide deluge, other than the life forms saved by the Ark of Noah, is a far-fetched narrative and is only mythologically sound. The concept that all humans are related to a common ancestor, Noah, can be offensive, objectionable, and unthinkable.

Everything in our society and secular world has standards. A standard is a basis which organization of life can refer to as a point or accepted position of reference—the final authority—the supreme court of life. Religion is no different. It also has its absolutes, its standards. If you are a Moslem, then the Koran would be your standard, Islam your faith. Certain individuals in America, when asked if they are religious, are quick to reply, "Yes. Do unto others as you would have them do unto you," or "Do unto others before they do it to you." Again a philosophy of life and a standard of living irrespective of any church affiliation. It is even possible to be religious about religion. How you, the reader, react to the content of this book will be based upon some religious or secular understanding.

The standard for Bible-believing Christians can be summed up in the statement, "God said it, I believe it, that settles it." Or better yet, "God said it, that settles it, whether we believe it or not." God is our authority and His Word is our standard.

Part II of this book was submitted by Dr. Walter Brown at the request of the author. It is a new look at Genesis and science. It is our joint desire to strengthen and expand your faith and to equip you with answers to how life, the earth and the universe began.

This book is not a solo effort. Many have helped in its preparation. Special thanks:

To Ed Davis for allowing the author to tell your story. For all the many interviews, telephone conversations, and use of your personal photographs and artifacts. For allowing the readers to share your experiences as you climbed Mount Ararat and viewed Noah's Ark.

To Dr. Walter Brown, who contributed Part II of this book. For all your many years of research. For boldly debating, lecturing and conducting educational seminars throughout the nation on science and the Bible.

To Jack Rex, friend and vice-president of F.I.B.E.R., without whose help and support this book would not have been possible.

To Dave GuMaer, the investigative reporter, for sharing your information and sketch regarding the missing Russian photographs.

To Richard Bryman, Bill Crouse, Dr. Jim Davies, Pat Frost, Al Jenny, Max Lare, Bill McGlone, John McIntosh, John Mulhern, and Dr. Max Wilson, for their special expertise and significant contributions.

All Biblical quotes used in the text are from the King James Version.

Photograph Credits

Dr. Howard Davis: pages 78 to 83, 84B.
Ed Davis: pages 51, 52, 53, 54A, 55, 56, 57, 58, 59, 60, 64 to 73.
Dewitt Hutson, page 54B.
All other photographs are by Dr. Don Shockey.

Part 1

The Ed Davis Story

Chapter 1
The First American to View Noah's Ark

The telephone rang and finally Ed answered. "Have you really climbed Mount Ararat and looked upon the Ark of Noah?" I asked. "Yes," he answered, "and I've never spent a more miserable time in my life than when I was on the mountain."

The conversation lasted some fifteen minutes, and after a future date had been agreed upon for a personal in-depth interview, I sat back in my chair reflecting on what Ed had shared with me. I tried sorting out the hundreds of questions I hadn't had the opportunity to ask. Can this be true or is it another false lead? My initial enthusiasm began to be tempered by cautious optimism. Why hadn't this information been made available for the last forty-two years? Would Ed's account leave so many gaps and inconsistencies that it would be yet another questionable, unverifiable, eye-witness report?

Just a few months before, Eryl Cummings, the dean of all ark-hunters, and I traveled to Arkansas to interview a man who claims to have seen a U-2 photograph of some large structure thought to have been the Ark on Mount Ararat. Then only a few weeks ago I flew to Phoenix, Arizona and talked with yet another man who examined the lost Russian photographs of the Ark taken in 1917. Unfortunately, most drawings do not include meaningful diagnostic landmarks precise enough to pin-point an exact location of the structure on the mountain. The mountains of Ararat can not be compared to any other mountain group in the world. Greater Ararat is nearly 17,000 feet high with four major glaciers covering its upper regions. It is one of the largest mountains in the world and is referred to as "the painful mountain" by the Turks.

As it turned out, the timing couldn't have been better. Dr. Howard Davis, my close friend and fellow Ark researcher, who has climbed Mount Ararat on five different expeditions, would be in Albuquerque and participate in the interview.

Ed Davis made us feel very comfortable and at home. He's one of those unusual personalities that project a warmth, a sincerity that you immediately feel. Ed was asked to begin his story, just as he lived it, and we would try not to interrupt, saving our questions until the end. The following is Ed Davis's story:

I was a member of the United States Army Corps of Engineers during World War II, stationed at Hamadan, Iran, building roads and supply routes into Russia. One of our local drivers was a young man raised in a small village at the base of Mount Ararat. On clear days, the towering peak of the mountain can be seen from the Iranian side. He went by the name of Badi.

Working together on the various projects gave us an opportunity to talk a lot. Badi told me of the many times he and his family had visited the wooden structure, Noah's Ark. The Ark was a very sacred and holy relic to them, and it was their family's responsibility to guard and protect it from outsiders. I became very interested in what he was telling me. Badi informed me that his father was the authority in his village and whatever he spoke, everybody must obey. He was the patriarch. All his family were very devout Moslems.

On one occasion Badi's father, who was around eighty years old came to Hamadan to visit his son. I gave the old man many pounds of English coffee which he appreciated. The old man and I both had an interest in horses and spent a lot of time, even with the language barrier, discussing the various attributes of American horseflesh versus the Persian varieties. The old man's name was Abas-Abas and his grandfather had been a soldier in the Iranian-Persian cavalry. Even though we were from two different cultures, two different backgrounds and religions, we liked each other and became friends. I was surprised when the old man gave me a leather canteen, which I still have, that he had used until 1917 when metal canteens were manufactured and first made available.

One thing led to another and he began telling me of the artifacts he and his family had found scattered on the mountain after a section of the Ark had broken off. I saw and held some of these artifacts Abas-Abas was now describing in his village before my climb up Mt. Ararat.

When I arrived at his village he showed me a door to a cage, all petrified, which I estimated to be about thirty to thirty-six inches high and about forty inches wide. This door had been broken off from some type of cage. I then was shown many latches that were used to lock the various pens, cages or compartments in the vessel. The old man told me that at certain times of the year, but not necessarily every year, portions of the Ark would be visible and could be seen protruding from the ice, snow, rocks and dirt. Abas-Abas told me that a piece of the back section had broken off, but when he was a youngster, it was more or less a complete boat, in one piece. Both Abas-Abas and his family have recovered pottery vessels at the site and some were found to still contain honey. In other containers they found dried beans and something that looked similar to lentils. Other edible food the Kurds recovered were some dried beans with the stems still attached.

Abas-Abas re-emphasized how sacred all these artifacts were to him and his family. "Many come to the mountain but few, very few, ever see. We always know who is on the mountain. God hides the structure from those who are not worthy to look upon it. A veil, a shroud of clouds God makes to cover it," he said.

These were the things the old man told me about, when I first met him. I saw most of the items from the Ark later at his village home.

During the summer of 1943 Abas-Abas returned to Hamadan and said the Ark was visible. His sons had just returned from the mountains and it was exposed. "We can go see it now." I asked my company commander if there was a way he could give me permission to take some time off and make the climb. My commander said that he'd give me some leave time and would figure out something to cover my absence. There was another boy in the chaplain's office we first thought would go with us, but the next morning when I went by to pick him up, he had decided to go to Tel Aviv for R and R (rest and recuperation). I loaded up my army truck with three extra barrels of gasoline and an extra case of motor oil and left Hamadan with the old man to drive to his village.

Abas-Abas's home near the base of Mount Ararat looked like a walled dirt compound. It was for protection of the animals; they brought them inside the walls every night and locked the gate. Everybody lived with him in this house—Abas-Abas's wives, daughters, his mother, his grandmother and all the girls and their babies up to seven years old. Boys at seven go to where the men live. Inside his home was an upper loft, very long, like an inside porch, and one would have to climb some steps to get to the upper level. The majority of their living, cooking, and eating was done downstairs and their sleeping upstairs.

It was at this time that the old man gave me a cup, a blue cup, a bowl and a spoon. I carried my own Army knife. Abas-Abas told me to keep them as they would be needed for the mountain trip. I tied these eating utensils on a cord and threw them over my pack and neck. Each person had his own gear for eating. Inside his home I saw a big pot containing some type of stew hanging over a firehearth on a swinging arm. It had everything in it including meat and lots of vegetables. I was served some bread with the meal and was offered some dried fruit in another bowl. On a wooden ledge were dried onions, dried herbs and more dried fruit from which you could help yourself at any time. The old man gave me such a big serving that I had to pour part of it back into the main pot. We then went to bed and everybody slept together.

Sometime around midnight someone was knocking at the door and yelling very loudly, "We go! We go!" We left and another one of the old man's sons joined us from his house. We drove in a truck, a British Morley, as far as we could drive. The roads were bad, and I think about 9:00 that morning we arrived at the first camp that would serve as our base of operations. There we were joined by about eight of his family, all men. It was at this camp that horses were provided. We packed the horses and rode for what seemed forever. I was so stiff I could hardly move when we dismounted at our first cave to spend the night. Here we left the horses. From this point until we got to the Ark was on foot.

It began raining. Day and night it rained. You would take two footsteps and then slide back one. You've been on the mountain, Don. You know what it is like. We hiked all day, starting that morning from the cave where we had left the horses. Each had a canteen of water, jerky, dried fruit and bread the Kurds had brought with them. Everything was wet. Cold, miserable and wet. Finally, arriving at the next camp, which was also a cave, was a welcome relief. It continued raining all night and was still raining the next morning, forcing us to remain in camp for a long time. I don't know how long it delayed us.

Up on the mountain in this area you are walking in the clouds and fog all the time. The Kurds knew where they were going but I certainly didn't. The trail here wasn't too bad. It looked like it had been pretty well traveled. They told me we weren't taking the route that most of the explorers would take. It was sort of a backdoor route up the mountain. We were on the trail that banditos and marauders travel. It was harder but much shorter. They told me that the easiest trail up Ararat was more toward Russia but it is dangerous to let the Russians see you. The showed me two Russian out-posts in the far distance and were very, very careful not to get too close to any of them and be spotted.

It was still raining hard. During this third day, part of this trail had smaller rocks and gravel, smaller stones and we didn't slide off as often and made a little better time. This was the day we arrived at the final cave located near where we first looked upon the Ark. This cave was very well hidden but not far off the trail. Unless you knew how to get there, you'd pass the cave and never realize it was there. Abas-Abas told me we should have made it from his village in two days, but because of the bad weather it had taken us three instead. The old man said that many times soldiers are on the trail, and if any soldiers were seen we would have to remain hidden in the cave. Some of the Kurds with our group served as observers and scouts to warn us if anybody was seen.

We then hiked near Doomsday Point. That's what Abas-Abas called it. We continued on to a point where we could first see the Ark. It first appeared as a huge rock formation covered by fog, which would move in and out. The main part of the boat was off to the northeast, to my right, and it was lying tipped over on its side. To my left and further down a slope about one-half mile, I could see a portion that had broken off from the main Ark itself. Both parts you could look into. Both of them had partitions, and cages.

Chapter 2
Questions and Answers

At this point of the interview, Dr. Davis and I could not restrain ourselves any longer and began asking the questions we needed to ask.

Don: Ed, about how far were you from the Ark at this time? Were you looking down or up at the Ark?

Ed: I was above the Ark looking down at it. I would say the main part was less than a mile away. There is another trail up above where we were. We were on the lower level. You'd need to drop down from the higher trail to where we were standing. That's where Doomsday Point is located. We had arrived in the afternoon (third day) and it had kind of let up raining, but the rocks were very slick and the only way to get down to the Ark was by ropes. Abas-Abas said we'd have to wait until the next morning to make the climb down, hoping the rain would stop and it wouldn't be so difficult and dangerous. The next day when we woke up, it was still raining. It rained most of that day.

Don: Ed, when you first viewed the Ark, about what time of the day was it?

Ed: It was in the afternoon.

Don: Where was the sun?

Ed: The sun was somewhere behind me, over my right side.

Don: It was somewhere behind you in the afternoon as you were looking at the Ark?

Ed: Right. At times you could see nothing but the clouds below.

Then they would clear and you could see the Ark itself. I believe it is the Ark. The Bible says it was there. It was a sea-going vessel and why would someone else place a boat here? That would be hard to believe. We had waited for a couple of hours before the clouds and fog lifted to get our first glimpse of the Ark.

Don: Do you have any idea the elevation you were at?

Ed: I have no idea. I knew at one time the elevation of the peak above us; the Kurd told me.

Don: Could you see the peak?

Ed: Yes, the big point was behind us slightly. There were clouds, we were in the clouds. All the ice was not completely melted out. The bottom part still had ice and I saw water running out of the Ark. Melting water was streaming down from the top and side also.

Don: What time of the year was this?

Ed: It was around the first of July. It starts getting warmer on the mountain around March or April.

Don: Did you go through a great deal of ice and snow before you arrived at the Ark's location?

Ed: No, not a great deal. Most of it had melted off the trail, but there was some in the ravines.

Don: Was the Ark located in a wide or narrow area, when you first looked upon it?

Ed: I could see an additional quarter of a mile beyond the Ark into more clouds and fog. The Kurds told me if it were clear they could see into Iran. It looked like a mass of hills or talus leading up to the mouth and the Ark was in one main abyss (canyon).

Don: Was there a drop-off from the canyon edge?

Ed: It wasn't far at all. It was lying in a cove like. You could see into the end of the Ark itself. It was partially melted out but not completely. [See drawing Ed made for me on paper, in section of illustrations.] The Ark was tipped, lying on its side, its right side. The living quarters, according to Abas-Abas, were at the top, close to the bow. The part that broke off was the back end.

Don: Describe it for us. Was it submarine shaped or more like a box? Did it have stories in it or what?

Ed: It looked like a solid piece of material which was at the bottom, a solid piece that ran clear up into the dirt, soil and rock. You couldn't see the complete front end. The compartments were on an angle and you could see all of the big beams that separated these compartments. The smaller compartments were high up, and the bigger ones down low toward the bottom. It must have had a second or third story. The living quarters were more or less in a raised compartment that stuck up above the general conformation of the structure.

Don: Judging its dimensions from your vantage point, how wide and high was it?

Ed: It looked over a couple of hundred feet, I really don't know. It was hard to judge. All I can say is that it was big. It was hard to make an estimate but there was plenty of room in there. The living quartrs looked relatively small up at the top. The Ark had a small superstructure that covered the living quarters. The sides looked slightly rounded from the bottom up to the top covering.

Howard: Would you describe the bottom structure and superstructure again?

Ed: There was a beam on the bottom and it was slightly rounded coming up the sides. Then you come to the top of the Ark which had another structure along the middle above the top. You could see inside this from the end which was broken off.

Howard: I am interested in the living quarters you described.

Ed: We could see the living quarters were above the animals' compartments.

Howard: The Russians who examined the Ark back during the First World War say that is had iron, metal bars on the cages. Did you see any of those?

Ed: Let me tell you, those iron bars were rock, petrified wood. I saw some of the cage doors [that the old man showed him in Ahora Village] and they were not iron. The ones I saw were petrified wood. The old man had some of these petrified wood latches off some of the cage doors at his house.

Howard: Describe one of the latches you saw for us.

Ed: Most of the latches were a piece of wood shaped like this [gesturing] and it was fastened with pins and holes in each piece. Then it had a long bar that slipped through. There were several different pieces, some of which I couldn't figure out. Then there were some shaped something like this [gesturing] that evidently they dropped something into. The latches and this door to the cage are rock. The old man told me that all the cages are completely petrified.

Don: What about the door to the Ark? Is it missing or still intact?

Ed: The huge door is still attached to the Ark. I didn't see it, but the old man pointed to where it is on the side tipped up and hidden from where I was looking. According to Abas-Abas, in some years it had been open and in others closed. His grandfather had seen the Ark when the door was held open by a large boulder.

Don: Does the door open outward or inward?

Ed: It is closed now. The door of the Ark opens from the bottom, outward and up.

Don: Would that be like a garage door opens?

Ed: Yes, he told me it pushes straight out at the bottom and is attached at the top, and it is counter-balanced in some manner. I have no idea how large the door is—I don't remember asking Abas-Abas its dimensions.

Don: Was it attached with metal hinges?

Ed: I don't know.

Don: Noah had metal workers in his day.

Ed: I don't know. I never saw any metal.

Don: What color is the petrified wood you saw?

Ed: Different colors. When you first look at the wood it appears like you can see through it on the edges. It has a sheen, transparent-like on its edges. In the middle it is similar to a gray. Then others have a reddish cast. Dark.

Howard: Did you see any of the wood that had pitch on it?

Ed: I saw several pieces that had pitch on them. They still use the pitch. It is cherished. They take some of the pitch and a sinew-like cord and heat it and mold the cord into it. Then this bag is wrapped in a piece of cloth. Little kids wear it.

Don: What other objects did you see that were removed from the Ark?

Ed: At the village, the old man has several shepherd's sticks that are also petrified. All the artifacts the old man had down at his village were found outside the Ark when it broke up. Abas-Abas told me when he saw the Ark for the first time that it was not in the same position it was when we observed it. He said it was tipped up about fifty feet higher than it is now. And it was upright. As the ice and snow melts, it undercuts it and it will move slowly to a new position. These people are very, very careful not to molest or disturb the Ark. There is a curse on anyone that cuts or breaks something from it. I was told if we got inside not to break or remove anything.

Don: It is a holy relic to the Moslem people.

Ed: The first thing they did when we arrived at the Ark was pray. Abas-Abas told me that when Mohammed returns a heavenly light will spotlight the Ark and shine over it. They are very religious about it.

Howard: You said that part of the Ark was covered up?

Ed: Yes, the extreme end. It looked like the talus of the hill had covered the front part of the Ark. They told me the front part was the portion that still remained covered. The living quarters were in that part. This is the end where the dirt has washed over it.

Howard: The broken part is where?

Ed: The broken part is sticking back of it. That is where the larger cages are, at the back, the part we were looking into that was exposed. We were standing in the vicinity near Doomsday Point looking down at maybe a 45-degree angle to see into the end of the main structure. A piece had broken off and you'd see the timbers sticking out of it also. As the ice melted, the water undercut this tail-end, and it was sticking out into the air and finally broke off. This part slid down at least another half mile away. The field glasses we had, with which we tried to look through fog and clouds, really didn't work very well.

Howard: I have been on the mountain when the clouds were so thick we couldn't see even ten or fifteen feet away. Ed, you mentioned its only being seen at certain times. Is it ordinarily covered with ice?

Ed: Ice and snow.

Howard: Did they mention if it were visible every year?

Ed: No, there are years that it doesn't show at all.

Howard: This all coincides with reports from history and the stories we've heard.

Ed: According to the old man, Noah and his family settled below. They spoke a different dialect. They spoke a different language from those that went to Iran and all over the world.

Howard: That's in the Bible also.

Ed: The descendants of Noah still live near the mountain and are of the old group. Information has been passed down through each generation. For years the old man's family has gone on this mountain to collect supplies and artifacts that have been in the Ark itself.

Howard: Are these Iranian or Kurdish people?

Ed: The Kurds and Lourds have raided many times. It is quite likely that they themselves have been responsible for banditry. When outsiders go up the mountain, they follow and watch their every move. Some individuals and groups have disappeared and never been seen again. Anyone they find dead they strip of clothes and equipment, and they throw the body down a crevice. They can't haul the body down. One of the boys told me about finding a couple of people that were dead. They took all their belongings. He then showed me the place where I could see two human legs sticking out of the ice. They must have been fifty feet straight down. No clothes, no shoes.

Don: Up that high the cold can chill you something terrific. Did you ever get warm?

Ed: I was never so cold for so long a time. The cold goes right to your bones. You can't get warm. Inside the caves it was fine. Everybody would strip off and we dried our clothes in front of a fire inside the cave. We all looked rather strange running around in our birthday suits.

Don: Did you use climbing equipment and ropes?

Ed: Yes, something that bothered me. They had excellent climbing equipment. It looked like they had heavy Alpine boots. Most of it came from being found on the mountain, either left by or taken from other groups. They had a supply of sleeping bags stashed in all the caves. We met other Kurds who were staying in the caves with us that had not hiked up with our group. Sometimes on the trail they would come out of nowhere to let Abas-Abas know that all was clear and to go on. This group is careful. They are aware of everything going on at all times.

Don: When did you begin using ropes?

Ed: We roped up immediately after we left the horses. They tied us all together. Eight of us. I was fifth in the chain, with three behind me. Abas-Abas was third. A loop was made in the rope and you put your left arm into the loop and over your head, and the rest of the rope laid over your right shoulder. A snug fit. Some wrapped a coil or two around their body. I didn't understand at first why they insisted it be done, but it was not very long until I realized that it was a necessary, life-saving procedure. Lots of time on the trail I couldn't see the guy in front of me or the one behind. At certain times on the trail we'd take the ropes off and space ourselves a good distance apart so we wouldn't kick rocks onto those below. Rockslides were dangerous. We did use some sharp pointed sticks for support. Abas-Abas gave each of us two, and they were about six feet long.

Don: When I was on the mountain I used my ice axe. Others used old ski poles.

Ed: I think three of our climbers had ice axes also. I didn't.

Don: It is so easy to twist an ankle. Good boots are absolutely essential. Howard Davis and I started wearing ours in Erzurum to try and get used to them before our ascent up Ararat.

Howard: Ed, you mentioned jars with honey in them. Were there any other jars you saw at the village?

Ed: Yes, they had other jars from the Ark. There were some pots, bowls and types of water pitchers.

Howard: Do they look like shapes you've seen over in that part of the world today?

Ed: They are similar to what you can see over there today. One was shaped like a honeycomb and at the top were round holes. Maybe it was a reservoir for fresh water and it could be hung up. Abas-Abas's family found lots of strange bird feathers in the smaller cages toward the front end and in the highest level toward the top of the Ark. Also fish remains—nuts and shells.

Howard: Did you see any tools from the Ark that were at the village?

Ed: The old man showed me some pieces of metal that had a hole in them. I judged they were hammers. He also had one that could have been for splitting wood; it was wedge-like and also had a hole in it.
Don: Did the old man give you any artifacts from the Ark?
Ed: No. All of them are very sacred to Abas-Abas and his family. At the time I didn't realize how privileged I was to have just seen them.
Don: Did you pass any pools of water, lakes?
Ed: There were lots of pools of water that would melt and collect.
Don: Did they give names to identify landmarks as you were climbing?
Ed: None. I was fifth and roped up, and the Kurds on either side of me didn't speak much English. The high cave, according to Abas-Abas was about three kilometers, I think, to Doomsday Point. It would take three hours to hike from the last cave to the Ark and some three hours back.
Howard: You started up from the Iranian side to where the gorge comes out on the side of the mountain? You came around the bottom and then up the west ridge?
Ed: Yes, pretty far to the west. We came to this area under the highest point. Do you know where that is? We came west of there and past that down to Doomsday Point. Don't ask me directions because we couldn't see far off due to the heavy cloud cover on the mountain.
Howard: We have been in the area several times and I can follow your trail. We made one trip into this area probably at this point or near this point you're talking about, because the fog was so heavy we couldn't see more than ten feet in front of our face.
Ed: While walking in the clouds sometimes you would get a heavy smell. Sometimes it would be like rotten eggs and at other times a very sweet smell.
Howard: When you first came out of Iran, how long did it take you to get to the village?
Ed: I really don't know how far we were from the Russian border. The old man had told me, but I know we were very careful not to get too close. We had driven winding roads to get there.
Howard: It took you about three days to climb to the Ark?
Ed: Yes, but it took us about five days to come back down. We were cold and wet, and the extra clothes that I took were just as wet as the ones I was wearing. When we would get back to a cave, they would give us a sheepskin and then pull all our clothes off and dry them.
Don: Did you observe any crosses or writing on the walls of these caves?
Ed: There was writing everywhere, and beautiful art work. General-

ly it would be a lion. The lion would be standing on its back feet, and a man would be standing beside it with a knife in his hand.

Don: Was there any funny looking old writing?

Ed: Lots of the writing had eroded and sloughed off onto the floor of the caves. All the caves had writings on the wall. Some of it was red-looking, almost like pottery.

Howard: Do you ever recall seeing Lesser Ararat or the smaller peak?

Ed: A time or two when the clouds would separate and move out, they'd say, "Aja, Aja."

While we were standing near Doomsday Point a piece of the mountain collapsed and started a rockslide. We watched it go down the mountain.

Howard: Where you climbed, were you on the rocks?

Ed: It was a pretty well-beaten trail. One place we got to, you could see that it had been cut off, leveled off, and we went around in the direction that the mountain had broken off.

Don: Do you know if spikes were used in the construction?

Ed: According to the old man, Noah used wooden pegs, not spikes. This I can't personally verify. It was what he told me. When the Ark broke off it may have been at a splice joint. The old man had no reason to lie to me. They took very good care of me at all times.

Don: Were any photographs taken of the Ark?

Ed: I doubt if they would have allowed me to take a camera even if I'd had one. It would open a can of worms, because they are trying to keep the Ark hidden since it is holy. Unfortunately, there wouldn't have been any real chance to use one due to the constant storm we found ourselves in. It was only for short glimpses we could see through the rain, clouds and fog. You've been on the mountain. You know what I mean. That mountain is different from any other place I've been.

Don: Have you seen any photographs of the Ark?

Ed: No, but the old man told me that some good ones have been taken by someone, Swiss or German, years and years ago and that he would try and get me a copy that he would bring to Hamadan later. This never happened because I was transferred to duty with General Patton's group in Europe.

Speaking of pictures, I want to show you some interesting pictures I have of my stay in Hamadan, Iran. Meeting the Shah and his first wife was a very big thrill for me. I was a member of a group of G.I.'s who were invited to the Royal Palace in Tehran for a party. The Shah's wife was the sister of King Farouk of Egypt. She asked me many questions about America. We were shown their stable of horses. As it turned out, the Queen's favorite horse was lame, so I took a look at the lame leg and discovered a small nail or piece of metal that was embedded in the soft flesh of its hoof. I removed it. The Queen was so grateful that she removed the gold earrings she was wearing and gave them to me. I still have them in my collection. I liked the Shah's brother George very much. He was interested in what New Mexico and the Wild West was like. He'd heard about our Indians and cowboys. I tried to set him straight about what New Mexico was really like. George and I went on several wild hog hunts while I was stationed in Iran. I have one of the hog hides in my storage shed. George even gave me his personal dagger which has a silver handle and Damascus steel blade. I guess I got off the subject. I'll get back to the Ark.

Don: Ed, you said that the Ark was in a narrow canyon. What else do you remember about its location?

Ed: Yes, it's in a small draw or canyon on a ledge. We didn't go anywhere else. We were waiting to go down on the rope. Abas-Abas, the old man, told me that at certain times, in certain years, all the Ark is visible. They laughed about all the fuss people have had trying to get to it. There was another ledge above the ledge we were standing on. The main trail goes along that upper trail. They called it Camel Back at the extreme top.

Don: How far above you was the upper trail?

Ed: About three-fourths of a mile.

Don: Anything else?

Ed: The old man told me that when he was a youngster a couple of climbers were caught in a terrible storm, snow, ice, et cetera, and were forced to spend several nights inside the Ark itself. They got very ill. A type of lung infection, emphysema like. There is some type of mold or fungus, bluish-white, that grows at times on the structure.

Howard: Tell us about this stone artifact you have.

Ed: I found this stone knife in one of the caves we slept in on the mountain. This cave had lots of ledges in it, and one morning I was looking across and something caught my eye, a reflection from the fire I guess. It looked whitish. I couldn't just jump up and get to it so I fooled and messed around. Then when I had a chance I went to the ledge and reached up. The first thing I touched was a lot of bird crap, but I felt farther down and found the stone knife. Back to the Ark. That afternoon we were sitting in the cave drinking some tea. The old man said we may have to wait two days until it was safe to go down to the Ark. If we started a rock slide, this part of the mountain would go. It stopped raining for a while that afternoon and the sun came out through some holes in the coulds. Abas-Abas thought that probably the next day would be a good time. About 10:00 that evening it began snowing, and it snowed all night. By noon the snow was above our knees, and they said we'd better get off this mountain now. We had to leave then.

Howard: This was in July?

Don: What an experience you had, Ed!

Ed: We were so close, but I'm still tickled to death that I was able to see it, and to see what I saw.

Don: People have been searching all their lives and never viewed it.

Ed: Did you and your group see anything?

Howard: No, we had guides with us, but we had to go where the guides took us. We couldn't go off on our own. One time we were able to go without the guides on our own for about three days, but we were over on the glacier, which was west of where you were.

Ed: Didn't the Russians run you off?

Howard: It's outside of Russian control, but they do complain and protest our being on Mount Ararat. They watch everything with telescopes and binoculars. They don't want us up there.

Ed: When the old man told us to go, we left, and it took five days to get down to the village again. I was cold and miserable.

Don: Ed, have you ever talked to anyone else that has climbed Mount Ararat?

Ed: No, you are the first. Everybody asks me, where is Mount Ararat? What is it?

Don: Have you ever read any books about Mount Ararat and the various searches for the Ark of Noah?

Ed: A lady showed me an article in something like the *National Geographic*, a special edition article, which told something about Mount Ararat, but she never sent me a copy of it.

Don: Basically, the only information you've had, other than the Bible, is totally from your own experience.

Ed: That's all.

Don: Who have you shared this information with? Did you think everybody had this information?

Ed: Nobody seemed very interested. After I came back from the war, and would mention it, their first question was, did you touch it? Did you photograph it? I'd say no. They would then give me the impression that I was sharing something like a flying saucer sighting. I would just drop the whole thing. Nobody likes to be made fun of. I saw what I saw, and it was real. If they choose not to believe my experience, that is their problem, not mine. I wish Abas-Abas had gotten the picture to me. If the other Americans at the chaplain's office had gone with us, then there would have been another to substantiate the climb and sighting. I consider myself very lucky to have seen it. People now would have to ask me to share it, otherwise I wouldn't bring the subject up. I'm glad you know what I'm talking about.

Chapter 3
Follow-Up Interviews

Following the initial interview with Ed Davis I have had numerous phone conversations with him and visits in his home, gathering additional information. He continues to recall other items he didn't mention at our first meeting. He is a very remarkable individual. What follows is an explanation he gave about the drawing he made of the Ark as he viewed it in July, 1943. Place Ed's drawing (see page 87) in front of you to follow his explanation as given below:

Here is the contour of the land. It was lying on its side, and this would be the bottom of the Ark and this was a sort of keel at the bottom. This small sketch in the upper left is what you would see looking at it from the side. The timbers are sticking out here and down there. The old man told me where the door of the Ark was located. It is over on the opposite side. The old man said it is shut now. It is about halfway between this end and the end which you couldn't see, almost in the middle. This other end is in the rock and snow. That is the front end of the Ark according to Abas-Abas. This was the part I couldn't see. This other end stuck out as the snow and ice melted and it was undercut and broken off. Water is coming out of the back end, here. The living quarters are here at the top with the structure extending above.

I asked Ed, "Where would Doomsday Point be located on your drawing?" He answered:

Doomsday Point is down there, to the lower left. A huge rock is up above on the next rim, on the ledge above it. That's where the good trail is located and where most of the explorers travel. Abas-Abas said you can't see where we are from that trail, and it is almost impossible to come down here off of that upper trail. The old man's grandfather told him that the Ark in his day was not where it is today. Then it was some fifty feet or more higher up, and the Ark door was open. And it was upright, not tipped on its side. The sun would be west, here. It was hard to judge the few times the sun peeked through the clouds and fog.

There has been erosion. There are a rockslide and ravine between the broken piece and the main structure. It probably slid or was shaken across after it broke up. This ravine is here to the left. We were standing between Doomsday Point and the ridge looking down. Doomsday Point was the drop-off.

A few days before Christmas I received a phone call from Ed. He had finally located the Bible he had carried throughout the war. Written on the back leaf was a brief account of his trip up the mountain. He had hidden the Bible in such a safe location that he hadn't even seen it for the last fifteen years. Ed had told me at our second meeting that if he could locate his Bible, it contained some notes about his experience on the mountain. It was a deeply spiritual experience for him to write and record an account documenting the event. He said to me:

You are drawn much closer to God in wartime and even though the Bible is beaten-up and coming apart, it is very precious to me. I have other notes about my discharge and events that later happened when I was in Europe and with General Patton. God knows that it is the truth.

To Ed this Bible was his peace of mind and security throughout all the dangers and battles in which he participated. This is what is recorded by Ed Davis in his Bible following his return to Iran from Mount Ararat. The spelling is exactly as he wrote it:

Went to Ararat with Abas. We saw a big ship on a ledge in two pieces. I stayed with him at the big house. It rained and snowed for ten days. I stopped in Tarharan and got some supplys and got warm and rested up. Also some new clothes.␣␣Lt. Bert was glad I got back. He was scared for me. He was afraid I would get killed I think. I am glad I went. I think it is the Ark. Abas has lots of things from there. My legs are almost healed from the horse back ride.

The Bible had been given to Ed at Camp Park, Hamadan, Iran by the chaplain Paul A. Barker of Haleyville, Alabama.

During the subsequent visits with the author Ed would always have some additional information or some rememberance that he had forgotten to share previously. Notes were taken and this is condensed in the remainder of his story. Ed continues:

We were all roped together. I was fifth in the line. Two Kurds walked behind me at all times. I guess they were like my bodyguards. If I made a bad slip, they were immediately trying to help me. I could tell that his group of climbers had made this trip many times. They knew exactly where they were going even in the dark. They must have made this trip many, many times. They told me they had. I felt more than a little strange being the only American on the trail. When we would stop, I would make the coffee. I had carried two five-pound cans of British coffee with me, and that set me up real good with them. I mixed the coffee. One of the Kurds had tried several times but he would either make it too strong or too weak, and we couldn't drink it that way. From that point on I made sure it was measured right. It seemed to me the coffee was a welcome change over all the hot tea (chi) they usually drank. They would wake me before sun-up to have it ready. Then the Kurds would put it on the fire and fix our breakfast. We did eat fairly well. Lots of jerky, dried fruit, some nuts and lots of parched corn. It surprised me that they would boil most of their water before drinking it. I thought they were probably accustomed to all the germs and bugs by now. It didn't help me, because on the trip back off the mountain I got sick. It had bothered me why I had written in the Bible, when I returned to Tehran, that I got some new clothes. This was the reason. By the time I got back to the company barracks, I smelled so bad that they made me burn my clothes and ordered me to bathe. I kept my billfold and belt. The Kurds had given me a belt, which I'll show you. It was made from Russian leather and was very fine leather. It still feels and looks good today. The buckle was hand-made. No brads were used, and they fastened the loop with a leather string knot. We can't even make one today that can hold together this well. I'll show you some wool socks the ladies at the village gave me. I took my army issue off at the camp, where we picked up the horses, and wore them on the mountain. They were warm, and I'm sure glad I had them. They must have given me three or four pairs. The colors in the socks are dyed, using all natural colors and pigments. I had saved my cigarette allowances for some time and brought these with me and gave them all to the Kurds on the mountain. My pack weighed somewhere between fifty and fifty-five pounds I'd guess. I didn't have any really special equipment other than my G.I. issue. The Kurds and Abas had good equipment. They acquired it from raids or it was found on the mountains. All of the climbers were given an aviator-type goggle by Abas. We wore them most of the time. You keep asking about landmarks on the trail up to the Ark. I remembered that on the second day hike Abas stopped and pointed up to a point above the trail we were on and said something I didn't understand. After a while I put my fingers together in a cross and he shook his head up and down, yes. It was a cross. I couldn't see what he meant, unfortunately, because the rain and fog were too bad at that point. I wondered if it were crosses carved on the rock or a rock formation that made a cross. This probably won't help you very much, but I just recalled that incident.

Abas gave me a piece of shiny metal that we could signal with. I never once had a chance to use mine. There wasn't enough sun for it to work. Abas also gave each of us a hand-operated flashlight we used in the cave. We squeezed it very rapidly, and it would generate enough electric current to light the bulb. I ended up bringing this back with me to the States at the end of the war. I carried all these items in my gear bag. The Kurds even had a bigger flashlight which you turned with a crank. They would signal each other with this one also. They never yelled or used loud voices at any time. I was given a small whistle to blow if I needed to get their attention. It sounded like a bird call. It wasn't like our police whistle. I brought it back with me, but I guess I've misplaced or lost it somewhere.

When we walked from Doomsday Point to the spot where we viewed the Ark, there was whispered talking. There was a reverance, and awe. You could feel like someone was watching your every step, every minute. Everyone treated the Ark like the holy relic it was. Everything got very serious, especially after we started the climb up from the second cave. Abas told me he hated anyone that went up exploring and searching for the Ark. He said everyone wants to get a piece, chop it up and carry it off. It was Abas and his family's responsibility to protect it from harm and exploitation, even if it meant killing.

Abas described another small opening or door that opened to the outside of the Ark. I don't recall his telling me where it was, but he called it by the same name they use for toilet hole. He said the people on the Ark used it to dump and remove the animal waste into the water. I wish I had asked him more about it but didn't at the time.

The Kurds would urinate on their hands and rub it in. I never saw one of them that had any problem with their hands. It must work. I never adopted that custom. It kept their skin from chapping.

Abas has crosses made from the petrified wood of the Ark at his home. They were hanging up in several places on the wall. They put several pieces together to form a cross.

You've been asking about more details of the living quarters of the people on the Ark. They were under a canopy and were about eight to eight-and-a-half feet high from the bottom to the top. As I told you before, this superstructure didn't extend all the way from the front to the back of the Ark. From the top deck, the canopy rose about knee-high to Abas and then went down the rest of the way to a floor. Abas showed it was a man's height with his arm extended as high as it would reach. The canopy or superstructure covered about one-third of the width. About one-third remained on either side to the edge. Abas counted some forty-eight compartments here. Guess some were used for sleeping, some for storage, or whatever. Abas and his family have found what looked like the pantry or kitchen area in the front of the Ark, the front end under the living quarters I just described. Here they have found everything from beans, the honeycombs, the nuts and shells, to dried fish bones and such. You and I talked about Abas and if his family ever saw a firepit or fireplace located aboard. I did ask Abas about this and he said no, no fire on the Ark. I did see at his home some pottery vessels that were about seven or eight inches long, kind of like the shape of a boat and opened in the middle. A container. I agree with you that they would have been oil lamps. You may be right that they may have cooked with oil. Who knows.

Speaking of food and eating, Abas described to me the method Noah used to water the animals. Do you know what they used? They used animal stomachs sewn together. Abas says there are many, many of these on board the Ark. They are still there. I didn't see any of these because they have never carried them down off the mountain. They were leather watering troughs, all different sizes and shapes.

I was very disappointed that I couldn't walk and explore inside this Biblical treasure. I had an overwhelming desire to touch it, something I can't explain.

I have this picture of the village and camp that Abas gave me. I wish he had given me a photo of the Ark, but he never showed me one or offered one even though he told me where two are located. This village of Abas's could be like Old Town in Albuquerque. Mud and rock construction.

I gave my wife a Persian lamb cap and a wooden inlaid box the women make at the village. They trade these items for salt, dried fruit and other food products. This jewelry box is lined with soft, white wool. They couldn't do enough for me and I was very appreciative.

I wish I could go back and visit them just one more time, but that will never happen. My health won't allow it. To the best of my recollection, this has been exactly what happened to me on Mt. Ararat. It's been a long time, but I'll never forget this experience. I hadn't realized that so few have ever seen the Ark. I hope the information I have given you will be of some help. I certainly hope so.

Chapter 4
Description of the Ark

At a later meeting with Ed I specifically asked him again to describe the smaller superstructure located on the top deck of the Ark. How long was it? How wide? Did it extend the entire length of the top deck? How far was it from each side? Ed related that, since he was some distance away, he couldn't make any kind of accurate observation, but it definitely did not extend to its bow or stern or full width. The width he could observe, but the length he couldn't tell, since one end was broken off and the other end was still encased in ice and debris. The top deck was receded back from the end he was looking into. Ed did ask Abas how high it extended above the deck and Abas answered him by holding his hand to his knee. Abas showed him that it was only knee high. I then asked Ed how tall Abas-Abas was in comparison to his height in 1943. He was shorter than Ed was, about five feet ten inches tall. Ed was around six feet, so Abas's knees came up about twenty-five or twenty-six inches.

Today we are not familiar with the scriptural dimensions and unit of measurement used by Noah, which was the cubit. The Ark was to be built 300 by 50 by 30 cubits, according to Genesis 6:14-16. In ancient times there really was no exact standard that the cubit represented. It could vary from country to country and from one location to another. One of these was the elbow or common cubit. This measurement was the distance from the elbow to the end of the extended middle finger. Egypt had its own. Here the cubit was the length of a new-born baby. This author had to get his yardstick out and determine what a Shockey cubit would reveal. My elbow cubit was nineteen inches. My new-born grandson's length at birth was nineteen and one-half inches. The author's knee measurement is twenty-one inches based on his five foot eleven and one-half inch frame. The point being that even though the cubit was a common unit of measurement used for the Babylonians, Hebrews and Egyptians, today it is only conjecture on our part to identify exactly what unit the standard cubit was that Noah used in the Ark's construction. The debate will go on until the time the Ark is actually measured. Some have valid reasons for believing that the cubit was eighteen and one-half inches. Others are just as certain it is twenty-two inches, still others from twenty-four to twenty-six inches. Taking this one step further, the Ark can be anywhere from about 450 feet to over 600 feet in length. Whatever the final answer will show, it was certainly large enough to preserve what God chose to preserve from the Deluge.

This superstructure built above the top deck was about knee high, according to the old Kurdish gentleman. The biblical description states that, "A window shalt thou make to the Ark, and in a cubit shalt thou finish it above." Is this where the windows were located, and are the openings underneath this superstructure? Abas said it was here that air entered the Ark. He told Ed there were no windows on the Ark's outside edges. This conflicts with descriptions given by other reported sightings. Some of these sketches clearly show rows of windows arranged lengthwise on both sides of the structure. If this were the case, Noah and his family could have looked out from any of these "windows" to observe when land was again visible. If the windows were under the wooden canopy in the center section of the top deck, it would have been extremely difficult to observe what was occurring directly underneath the boat. Noah could not determine from this position visually when to disembark from his year-long cruise. The scriptures again log this event:

And it came to pass at the end of the forty days, that Noah opened the window of the Ark which he had made; and he sent forth a raven, which went forth to and fro, until the waters were dried up from off the earth. Also he sent forth a dove from him, to see if the waters were abated from off the face of the ground. But the dove found no rest for the sole of her foot, and she returned unto him into the Ark, for the waters were on the face of the *whole* earth; then he put forth his hand, and took her, and pulled her in unto him into the Ark. And he stayed yet another seven days; and again he sent forth the dove out of the Ark; and the dove came into him in the evening; and lo, in her mouth was an olive leaf plucked off; *so Noah knew that the waters were abated from off the earth.* (Genesis 8:6-11)

Could there be another special opening (window) not yet observed which Noah used for this purpose? Much speculation and debate concerning "the window" which Noah opened to release the raven and the dove constantly surfaces. If a singular window was constructed, then all the animals remained in darkness throughout the year they were afloat. This does not seem to this author to be a reasonable speculation. The "window" is no proof that it was the only window opening to the Ark's three-story interior. Some speculate that God placed all the animals into a state of suspended animation, a year-long hibernation, and that they wouldn't have needed any light. Again, we don't know, but this seems a very unrealistic assumption. God was the architect and engineer of this rudderless, sailless, and motorless boat, but God used Noah, and who knows how many other helpers, to accomplish His design. The author feels that Noah was given some latitude in how it was to be finished.

Noah had flexibility in implementing God's instructions with his own common sense and knowledge gained by his six hundred years of education and experience. The author cannot necessarily see God floating down a blueprint from heaven showing where every wooden peg, wooden splice, and cage door latch were to be placed. The light was to be let in from above through an indefinite number of windows, and they were to be constructed in a manner which would not destroy the compactness, symmetry and waterproof integrity of the Ark. The semantics of the original "to make" can be interpreted as "to finish." "And thou shalt finish the Ark at the upper side by the cubit." Apparently the superstructure on the top deck contained many openings and did not extend lengthwise from end to end. Nor did it extend more than one-third of its width.

Chapter 5
Fragmented Section of the Ark

What about the large fragment of the Ark that was described as being approximately one-half mile down a very steep slope and across a crevass from Ed Davis's original observation point? I had him describe this over and over again to record every minute detail he could remember. Between the main Ark itself and the portion which had broken off is a deep crevass or ravine like a cleft in the mountain. Ed could not elaborate on how deep this ravine is, since he was unable to get any closer than the spot where he looked down at it. Which direction it was oriented was unknown, but Abas told him it was the back section that had broken off. On previous trips Abas had examined it and found artifacts scattered between the two sections from the Ark's interior after the breakup. The smaller, separated section is resting upon a narrow ledge and abuts a narrow canyon with ice and snow pack covering the backside. It appeared to have a sizeable collection of water below the ledge, and it looked to Ed like a large amount of water was cascading on down the slope. From Ed's vantage point he described the melting snow and ice collecting to form a raging stream. This broken section was very big and bleak-looking with some very large beams extending into the air. He said:

The fog and rain would get so dense and thick that it would disappear. I was mainly concerned with the main portion, and my attention was focused on it. It was only for short periods of time that both sections were discernable. The group had hoped to climb down to this secondary section but were completely thwarted and prevented from accomplishing this due to the weather.

I then asked Ed if it would have been possible to look up and see the main section had they been able to explore the area around the fragmented section. Ed indicated that:

We could have seen it if all the weather conditions had been favorable both from the ledge and from the small flat area beneath it. The Kurds pointed to a very obscure trail that led around close to it. Again we would have needed ropes to drop off from above it down to this section. The end we could view was slightly raised upward. It wasn't lying flat. I don't think we could have gone straight down and across to it from where we were. There was this deep gorge between us. We would have needed to go around and jog back to it. Even then looking back up to the main section would have been difficult if you didn't know exactly where to look, even without the fog and rain problem.

Listening to Ed relive this experience never failed to excite me. Ed then added that, according to Abas, when the Master returned to earth, the Ark would be put back together in its original shape. Ed failed to ask Abas why this would be necessary.

In reviewing the various reported sightings and their different descriptions of the Ark's size, shape, orientation which Ed Davis had never read or even knew existed, I believe it is very possible that some of these sightings of the Ark have been the fragmented section and not the main structure itself. Ed's observations may very well hold the key to understanding possible contradictions in these other sightings, since they may have viewed the fragmented portion of the Ark from different vantage points. Earthquakes are a common occurrence in this part of our world. Just after my return to the U.S.A. from our 1984 expedition, a serious earthquake occurred just north and east of Ankara, Turkey and many lives were lost. Earthquakes, melting ice, and water can shift the wooden structure literally yearly. Ed then told me that there was a space underneath the main Ark itself that has been undercut by the melting ice and snow which may eventually allow yet another breakup of the back end. How much wood and even artifacts are yet to be found scattered and carried downward by the elements? Some of these rock-slides may uncover new clues to life on the Ark at the time of the great Deluge.

The Ark has pictorially been represented throughout history from a houseboat to a pointed submarine. Western civilization went wild with their graphic representations. Cartoons are only limited by the artist's imagination. If you visit the Hotel Ararat in Dogubayazit, Turkey, the following sticker (emblem) is used for their advertisement.

Mount Ararat has been depicted as the resting place of Noah's Ark on a large bronze coin struck some 1700 years ago at Apameia Kibotos in northern Turkey. It is interesting to note that this numismatic artifact is the only coin-type known to bear a Biblical scene. On the reverse side of the coin there are three parts in which the Biblical Flood story is represented. In the central portion Noah and his wife are inside the box-like Ark lookout underneath an open lid and an inscription composing three Greek letters (NΩE) (Noah) struck on the Ark's side. A bird (dove) with an olive leaf in its beak is seen having landed on the roof of the structure. To the right of center this coin shows Noah and his wife with their arms raised toward the sky in apparent praise and thanksgiving, having just been rescued from the Deluge. (Information from: "An Ancient Coin Depicts Noah's Ark," by Yaakov Meshorer in the Sept./Oct. 1981 *Biblical Archaeology Review*, pp. 38-39.)

Chapter 6
Noah's Food and Fuel Supply

Something the author has wondered about for a long time when reading the flood story in the Bible is, how much food did Noah store on the Ark? Both for the eight people and the thousands of animals. Abas-Abas told Ed that the personal food for the eight humans was stored in the front end of the Ark just beneath the living quarters on the top story. The Kurdish family has found much evidence of dried meat, fish, honeycombs, beans and lentils scattered within this area. Ed also remembers Abas's telling him that in this area of the Ark he personally counted some forty-eight compartments. The scripture does not record how much food and supplies Noah should secure on board. Did Noah know the exact amount he would need for a one-year cruise? How about enough for two years? Maybe this was left open for Noah to decide. Would Noah's faith have allowed him to lay in store supplies for an extended stay upon the flood waters even if it were for several years? Who knows. The scripture does not give us these details. God knows not only our daily needs, but our long-term and extended needs too; and he requires us to trust him hour-by-hour, and day-by-day. The scriptures teach us not to rely on our own understanding. Noah would have listened to the thousands of skeptics around him if he had relied upon his own understanding. There had never been a flood before. There come many areas of an individual's life when understanding must cease and faith takes over. Noah's faith found acceptance by God. I've also wondered if Noah's wife was responsible for stockpiling their pantry. Was there an inventory and ledger kept? Probably. Does it remain hidden in some compartment on the Ark yet to be discovered?

The four members of our 1984 expedition all had their individual minor objectives when the Ark was re-discovered. One member felt that Noah would have some account written or notched upon a wooden timber which recorded each day they were on board the Ark. The author was interested in observing the many fingerprints which may have been preserved by indentations in the pitch. Would it be possible to record and duplicate the individual prints of Noah and the seven members of his family? Eryl Cummings and the author have discussed at length many aspects of the logistics involved in supporting all the life forms present on the Ark for one year. Originally it was felt that upon its re-discovery and upon careful examination it would be shown that the water supply, and the necessary waste disposal mechanisms would be as modern as anything we have today. The eyewitness reports do not support these preconceived human theories and ideas. God apparently uses what we have available at the time of need in order to serve His purpose. God could have spoken the "word" and the Ark would have been instantaneously created. Again and again He uses humans to accomplish His divine purpose. Whatever amount of food was stored, it was enough to sustain Noah, his family, and all the animals on board.

After the Ark came to rest and the water subsided, Noah and his family left it to begin life anew. A new generation and period of man's existence had begun on planet Earth. God told Noah to be fruitful and multiply. Noah evidently took some of the stored supplies from the Ark to sustain them until new crops were available for harvest, yet Abas-Abas found evidence of some of Noah's food supply still on the Ark. Other members of his family, including his grandfather, reported similar discoveries. Life as the world once knew was buried and destroyed beneath those flood waters. A cleansing had occurred, and the earth was now clean and fresh. Did the family of Noah replace their old cooking and eating utensils with new pottery vessels? The women could have taken clay on board to fashion and mold a new service for eight. The old was behind them and the new age was begun. There are many questions left to our imagination which cannot be answered at the present time.

Did Noah have a fireplace or firepit within the Ark? Was it oil- or wood-fueled? A small crack of understanding has been revealed by Abas. His family has recovered pottery vessels very similar in appearance to oil lamps used for lighting in the Middle East for thousands of years. Ed Davis held one of those lamps and examined it prior to his climb up Mount Ararat. This was one of the pottery oil lamps removed from the Ark site.

The only understanding of the Flood and Noah's Ark of one individual I talked to recently was the humorous monologue given wide television coverage by comedian Bill Cosby. Ignoring the scripture does not make it any less important or make it go away. We cannot afford to have the ostrich complex and hide our heads in ignorance or disbelief.

Study to show thyself approved unto God, a workman that needeth not to be ashamed, rightly dividing the word of truth. (2 Timothy 2:15)

And saying, Where is the promise of His coming? For since the fathers fell asleep, all things continue as they were from the beginning of creation. For this they *willingly are ignorant* of, that by the word of God the heavens were of old, and the earth standing out of the water and in the water, by which the world that then was, being overflowed with water, perished. But the heavens and the earth which are now, by the same word are kept in store, reserved unto fire against the day of judgment and perdition of ungodly men. (2 Peter 4:7)

Paraphrasing this scripture clearly tells us that in the final days of earth as we now know it, men will *willingly* be ignorant and disbelieve the Biblical accounts of Creation, the Flood and the return of Christ. How are you willingly ignorant? Simply by not believing God's word.

Chapter 7
Verification

How does one go about verifying data—accounts of events only shared verbally with another? It is difficult, if not impossible to accomplish. What motive, what reason, would Ed Davis have to fabricate such a tale? Was it for monetary gain? Why would he wait until forty-two years later if this was his purpose? Was it for publicity?

Of course not. If these had been the reasons, his story would have broken a long time ago. His war record places him in Tehran, Iran, at the right time. The original photographs place him in the correct geographical region, again at the right time. The artifacts contained in his display case are Persian. Ed gave us minute observations concerning his hike to and from the Ark which could not have been excerpted from books. To anyone who has ever climbed Mount Ararat or has been a serious Ark researcher, his story points to the conclusion that he was on the mountain just as he related. Everything fits. The danger, the caves, the fog, the trails, the major landmarks, the village, the habits of the Kurds. There are no questionable voids. Ed's body language when describing the Ark was very convincing to this author. Ed would turn and position his body to orient himself in an exact direction before he would describe what he was viewing and where. His hands were gesturing as he relived this experience. Pointing this direction and that direction, Ed was not even aware of his mannerisms during his presentation. Body language does provide clues. If all this was a fabricated, memorized version it is highly unlikely he would have told the story so naturally in this manner. Every time without exception when Ed was asked to describe where the Ark was located when he first viewed it, he would orient his body and then begin his description.

One of the landmarks related by Ed Davis was the spring (Jacob's Well) located near Ahora Village. When the Kurds and Ed began their ascent from the village, only a relatively short distance, they came to a wide plateau. Here was located an altar, and each of the Kurds carried a small stone which he placed on top of the altar. Dr. Howard Davis had camped at this same location for three days during one of his expeditions, and by tradition the natives call it the location of the tomb of Jacob. Dr. Howard Davis further related that the Koran (loose translation) says:

Apparently Jacob came back from Egypt and that God told him to go to the Holy Mountain and he would go to this location and find water. It would be a barren rocky area but that Jacob would find this flat area with a meadow and reach down and dig and water would come forth.

Dr. Davis's group would dig a hole at this stop and they did have water to drink. It was pure water (mountain spring water).

Another possibility for the name Jacob's Well at this Ahora location is a story from a 4th Century author—Faustus of Byzantium. It tells the story of St. Jacob of Medzpin who had asked God for years to be allowed to view Noah's Ark. The following is the account given by Faustus:

> About this time the great Bishop of Medzpin, that admirable old man, tireless in the works of Christian truth, that chosen of God, Jacob by name, of Persian origin, set off from his city to the mountains or Armenais, that is to say, to Mount Ararat in the principality of Ararat and the canton of Cortouk. He was full of the graces of Christ and had the power to do miracles and marvels. Arriving at his destination, he prayed God most fervently to allow him to see the Ark of deliverance built by Noah—the Ark which has come to rest on that mountain at the time of the Deluge. Now Jacob generally obtained from God all that he asked. While he was climbing the side of the inaccessible and arid Mount Ararat, he and those who accompanied him felt thirsty from fatigue. Then the great Jacob bent his knees and remained in prayer before the Lord. At the place where he laid his head, a spring of water broke forth by which he and his companions quenched their thirst. It is for this reason that to this day that spring is called "Jacob's Well." Meanwhile, he applied himself zealously to catch sight of the object of his desire, and not cease to pray for it to the Lord God. Already he had arrived near the summit of the mountain and thoroughly exhausted as he was, he fell asleep. Then the angel of God came and said to him: "Jacob! Jacob!" He answered, "Here am I, Lord." And the angel said: "The Lord gives ear to your prayer and grants what you desire. That which you find beside your bed is wood from the Ark. There it is: I bring it to you: it comes from it. Henceforth, you will cease desiring to see the Ark, for such is the will of the Lord." Jacob woke with greatest joy, praising and thanking the Lord. He saw the plank, which seemed to have been peeled off a large piece of wood with the blow of an axe. Taking up what had been entrusted to him, he went back, followed by his companions in the trip.... and it is preserved to this day among them as the visible sign of the Ark of the patriarch Noah. (From *The Ark on Ararat*, Tim La Haye and John Morris, 1976, pp 17-18)

Chapter 8
Weather Conditions

Attempting to prognosticate the weather on Mount Ararat more often than not is a lesson in futility. As a rule of thumb, the optimum time of the year would be from the second half of July to the first half of August each year. Even if this time period is undertaken for the climb and exploration of Mount Ararat, it is certainly no guarantee that hazardous weather patterns will not occur. Weather conditions change like a cameleon's color from minute to minute. Starting out from camp early in the morning with a clear sky, spirits soaring, the adrenalin surging, visibility excellent and several hours later returning wet, cold, miserable and physically exhausted is normal. Once you've been on the mountain it is very easy to understand why it is called by the Turks, "the painful mountain." All your equipment must be carried, and it must be the proper equipment. These packs may weigh from forty-five to fifty-five pounds, and combining this with the thin air, working your way to the mountain's upper regions can produce startling physiological and phychological changes in the climber. Your mind is telling you to abandon some of the extra weight. Do I really need that extra camera, that bottle of petrol, the extra sweater and coat? You are constantly moving upward over boulder-strewn ridges and ravines, and when you come to a downgrade or flat stretch it is even more difficult to walk due to equilibrium conditioning. You seek out a small upgrade at this point to feel better.

Once you stop for a short rest it is twice as difficult to lift your pack and begin all over again. The fog can move in without warning, and at times you cannot see ten feet in any direction around you. Even in August, the so-called optimum time, the temperature has been known to drop to -40 degrees and winds can blow up to 100 miles per hour. Several feet of snow can fall in a matter of hours. Freezing rain, hail, and blowing wind tell your survival instincts you had better get off the mountain. It is a major chore to fix meals, and believe it or not, you're not that hungry most of the time. The expression of being too tired to eat fits Mount Ararat so well that weight loss will occur. Other explorers have been struck by lightning during the fierce electrical storms. Then come the glaciers and snow packs which present an entirely different approach to the exploration. Water freezes. You can get severe cases of sunburn and snow blindness. High altitude sickness takes its toll. The point I wish to make is that at best the mountain can be described as being totally unpredictable—weather-wise. Being pinned down for hours inside the cramped space of a two-man tent can be a lesson in absolute frustration.

The summer of 1984 found the mountain at one of its better times for exploration according to the Kurdish natives who live year-round near the mountain. The snow-line had receded more than normal. Unfortunately, it wasn't the weather that totally prevented our research team from accomplishing our goal in 1984; it was political implications. At one point around 15,800 feet we were told that we could go no further and must leave the mountain. We could not have permission to explore the north and northwest areas of Mount Ararat. Were we getting too close? Too close to what? The Ark? Too close to Turkish observation points? Too close to a Russian installation that might be visible through our binoculars? The disappointment was instantaneous. We Americans were visitors and must comply with the orders. No other alternatives were open. We had to climb down off the mountain and return home, even though several more weeks of exploration were granted by our special research permits.

With Ark hunters, failure is never final and there will be another year. Set-backs are the rule, never the exception.

Unfortunately, there is not a great amount of geological research data available about Mount Ararat. The Parrot, Abich and South glaciers are major landmarks. The twenty-two square mile icecap is hundreds of feet thick and flows down all sides of the mountain. The rugged terrain contains countless peaks, valleys, ravines, and crevasses. All mountaineers are familiar with the ever-present danger of thin ice bridges, or snow covering deep crevasses, only to be discovered at his ice axe hopefully finds them before the climber hurtles into the bowels of the mountain.

Most are aware of the volcanic eruption of Mount St. Helens in March of 1980 in Washington State. A similar eruption occurred in 1840 on the northeast side of Mount Ararat which was estimated to have removed one to two cubic miles of the mountain in one brief pyroclastic explosion. I observed car-sized boulders shot fifteen miles away from the source. Ahora Gorge was formed at this time, several miles long and thousands of feet deep and wide, deeper even than our magnificent Grand Canyon in Arizona. Now geologists and explorers can view what the original geological core contained. Because of the explosion, the best place to study sediments and rock specimens is in the Ahora Gorge area. Its exposed mineral specimens can be representative of the entire mountain. Smaller volcanic cones are present scattered around the area including a prominent volcanic cone, Lesser Ararat, near the Iranian border on Ararat's southeast side. Dr. Clifford L. Burdick, one of the few to perform serious geological research on the mountain, discovered that the main body is composed of grey-hornblende andesite covered with pumice. Some Olivene basalts and andesitic lava are scattered throughout Mount Ararat's upper regions. The only way pillow lava is formed is under water or snow. Just another evidence of the Deluge.

History records the origin of life in the Fertile Crescent, the area including the mighty Tigris and Euphrates Rivers' drainage system.

The Euphrates River has its origin on the south end of Mount Ararat. According to Dr. Burdick:

> Instead of Ararat forming a drainage pattern radiating from the mountain, the watershed drainage flows to the Aras and Tigris and Euphrates apparently as if it did not know that Ararat existed, thus suggesting a more recent birthday for Ararat. The original drainage system may have been established from the days of Creation. Everything about Ararat suggests youth.

Salt deposits are found in close proximity to Mount Ararat on the Turkish side and to the south and east on the Iranian side. At Tuzluca some fifty miles northwest of Mount Ararat is a 400-foot-thick salt deposit. Everybody is familiar with our San Andreas fault which is causing some serious concern about future earthquakes on America's west coast. The eastern section of Turkey has its own serious fault line. It comprises what is known as the East African Rift and its complex fault system. Generally speaking, this fault line runs in a north-to-south direction, according to Burdick, and encompasses three volcanic peaks. These peaks are Alaoz on the Russian side of the Aras, and Greater and Lesser Ararat in Turkey. Burdick further describes the volcanic extrusions along faults parallel to the triple peaks in the Tendurek Mountains to the west and southwest of Ararat. The Tendurek Mountains and Doomsday Valley have received publicity recently by a group which stated that this geological phenomenon is really the remains of the Ark of Noah. Most serious Ark researchers have dismissed this "object" from consideration. If this geological mud and lava flow captured any wooden structure, it is not Noah's Ark. The Ark is resting on Mount Ararat where Ed Davis saw it.

Would climatic conditions on the mountain permit observation next year or would the next decade find the elements so severe that the Ark would be completely encased in ice and snow and hidden from view? One plans for the worst then hopes and prays for the best.

In the author's files is a report written by Cecil A. Roy and published in the Bible-Science Newsletter of July, 1978, which attempted to analyze favorable or unfavorable weather conditions on Mount Ararat during the years of reported sightings of the Ark. Since no data were available from any point within 100 miles of the mountain, no empirical records can be researched. Mr. Roy did obtain data for general weather conditions for a 500-mile diameter region around the mountain to observe what general conditions were present during the years of reported sightings of the Ark. Both temperature and precipitation were studied resulting in four major groupings, Hot-Dry, Hot-Wet, Cool-Dry, and Cool-Wet, the premise being that when the sightings were reported, were the weather conditions on the mountain such that the Ark or portions of the Ark would be exposed? Keep in mind that only general information is available for whatever insight it may or may not suggest. It is not my purpose to list all of these sightings, not necessarily documented, because they are in print. From Mr. Roy's article he states that from 1941 to 1945 (World War II) there are four reports but no set dates for any of them. 1941 and 1945 were probable years with 1944 as a "maybe." He goes on to say that until further information is discovered, we can only say that conditions on Mt. Ararat were such that sightings could have been made. Mr. Roy summarized his data by stating that of the twenty-two reported sightings up to this time period, thirteen passed the climate test, and four might have happened (World War II). Three reports do not correspond with his theoretical probability format.

The Rev. James Brady of Pensacola, Florida, felt that Mr. Roy's "average" data would have been more realistic and acceptable to use "mean" based on temperature and precipitation to derive a base mark to show conducive years above the mean and non-conducive years below the mean. Rev. Brady stated that since the Ark sightings were reported in only 17 percent of the 79 years charted, it should be expected mathematically that a similar percentage of "conducive" years should contain sightings. In actuality, though, such sightings were reported in 30 percent, or nearly one-third of all years conducive to such, and only five percent of years when conditions would have made such sightings unlikely. (Bible Science Newsletter of Oct. 1978 by Rev. Brady)

Ed Davis's sighting was in July of 1943, and based on the information just listed, the weather conditions at this time could have allowed visible observation. The reader must keep in mind that weather conditions on the extreme upper limits of the mountain are entirely different and unique from those on the mountain a few thousand feet lower. The fact remains that conditions were such that Ed Davis was able to view the Ark that summer of 1943.

Chapter 9
Ed Behling's Story

Those who have been intimately involved with research on the Ark are very familiar with the accounts of Prince Nouri, Haji Yearam, George Hagopian, Chuchian, Vladimir Roskovitsky, George Greene, Fernand Navarra, Gregor Schwinghammer, and now Ed Davis. One particular sighting which bears additional consideration and re-evaluation belongs to Ed Behling, a clinical phychologist from Gunnison, Colorado. There are many similarities between his account and that of Ed Davis. Behling was working for the U.S. government in Turkey and was shown the Ark in 1973. I will give a synopsis of the details related by Ed Behling in an interview conducted by Pat Frost, Ararat explorer, and Dr. Emil Gaverluk of the Southwest Radio Church. Ed Behling said:

I climbed Mount Ararat with the aid of a very, very old Turkish shepherd. In fact, he looked like he had been dead for about five years and just didn't know enough to fall over. We were very close to the Russian border, so taking pictures might not have looked good. If I had had a camera with a Turk that close to the Russian border, someone could have gotten in trouble. There's ice and snow all over the place. We had a fairly heavy parka and snow boots on and it was chilly. The snow had melted quite a bit off the Ark so there wasn't very much on top, and there was nothing on the sides. On top of the cliff is a shelf, a big platform. It looks like God put the shelf there just to rest the Ark. The front end of the Ark is broken off with a gaping hole. It is hard to give you a mental picture of just how wide and how tall it is. I saw no doors at all, nothing that looked manufactured. I have no idea how something that large came to rest that high on Mount Ararat. I can't explain it. People can believe in evolution if they want. All they have to do is explain away what I saw! When I was up there, the clouds were low on the mountain. We could see at the maximum maybe 100 or 200 yards, because of the fog around us. It was kind of eerie, especially when I looked down over the cliff and saw the Ark. It was so dark and overcast late in the afternoon that we left the next morning, and we camped underneath it. I didn't have direct sun any time I was there, so the gaping hole that I saw was dark. The whole Ark was black. It was basically square. I don't know how long it was; but looking into the mouth where it was broken off on the edge of the shelf, I saw it was basically square. The walls were straight up and down on each side and the base, which I couldn't see because of the angle, looked fairly flat.

35

The ceiling was slightly tapered, maybe five or ten degrees, just enough so the water could run off. On top of that was a catwalk about ten to fifteen feet wide and six to eight feet high with a roof over it. I guess they walked on that or maybe it was used for windows, but that's the way it looked to me. Basically, it was a big box that was very long. I could see only 150 to 200 feet of it, and then it tapered off into the snow. One end was broken off and had a gaping hole. It was as if something had cut it in half. I was looking at only one section of it. The other end was covered with snow. I was looking at the end of the Ark. It was like somebody took a stick and broke it in half, and you looked at one end of it. That was the end I was looking at. The Ark was forty to fifty feet high and sixty feet wide. It was on the cliff about 100 fet above us so we could look up into the mouth of the Ark. The walls must have been eighteen inches thick. Remember, I was 100 feet below it looking up at it.

Unfortunately, Behling could not remember any specific landmarks, peaks, or starting directions to follow his trek up the mountain. Behling added, "I thought everyone had seen the Ark. That is why I haven't talked to anyone about it for the last eight years."

Chapter 10
Can the Information Be Trusted?

Bibles have been used to record significant information such as births, deaths, marriages, wills, baptisms, et cetera. When a person places his or her hand on a Bible in our courts of law, he takes an oath to tell the truth, the whole truth, and nothing but the truth. Information written in Bibles can be considered legal documents when additional authenticity or records are unavailable. Ed Davis's brief account was written in his Bible as his record of this most rare and spiritual experience. Viewing Noah's Ark was an encouragement to his faith, a support for his Christian beliefs. His account is very personal and real.

Why hasn't God chosen to let a professional surveyor, engineer, photographer, geologist, theologian, archaeologist, linguist or artist scientifically verify the existence of the Ark to the doubting world? I can't answer that question, but I have a very strong feeling that it is because of God's timing, not man's.

What information concerning the Ark's being on Mount Ararat was available in 1943? The first American expedition by Search, Inc. began in 1959, sixteen years later. Navarra, the French explorer had not made his discovery of wood on the mountain in 1943. It was in the summer of 1945 before the account of the Russian flyer Vladimir Roskovitsky's sighting at the end of World War I was published. George Greene's photographs and maps mysteriously disappeared and were of a much later date. The Bertha Davis photographs and their disappearance (no relation to Ed Davis) was in the '60's. The list could go on and on, the point being that information was very scant. No organized collection of data was available to the layman. Ed has shared his black-and-white photo of the village of Abas-Abas, his starting point for the climb.

Another very important factor is the reliability and credibility of the information the Kurds shared with Ed. Can their information be trusted? Again, keep in perspective that the year was 1943. World conditions were entirely different from what we find today. The Turkish people have historically been American allies and friends. Turkey holds a very strategic position in its geographical location. Air travel, transportation and commercial airports were in the infancy stage. The "Ugly American syndrome" was not yet prevalent.

The Kurds inhabit the countryside around Mount Ararat, living in very primitive conditions even today. Mr. Tom Jared of the 20/20 T.V. program described the Kurdish village of Dogubayazit, located on the southwest end of the mountain, when he visited it in the summer of 1985, as what Dodge City, Kansas would have looked like before Wyatt Earp. Dogubayazit is a thriving, modern metropolis compared to Aralich and Ahora Village. Imagine what it would have been like in 1943.

A family of Kurds did allow Ed Davis to accompany them to the Ark. Why? I cannot reveal the specific reason these villagers would be forever indebted to Ed Davis. It is a highly significant reason. Ed Davis requested that I not reveal these reasons until after his death. I will abide by his request and trust in me. What could the Kurds at the village do to possibly compensate and show their gratitude to Ed? They had very little resources. The family decided to share with him their greatest treasure, the Ark of Noah. This was the most important honor they could bestow. He was allowed to view the sacred artifacts taken from the Ark. If there was ever an adoption ceremony, this was it. They shared information as if he were one of their own. Ed Davis was a very important visitor. What greater honor could be given than this, their religion, their heritage, their village and family secrets? In 1943, Ed Davis accomplished a feat which apparently has not been repeated.

Terrorism is rampant across the globe. It appears to be open season on any American, anywhere in the world. The ugly head of violence and physical threats has been seen on God's special mountain, Mount

Ararat, this past summer of 1985. Two American research teams were held at gun-point, harassed and robbed. They may have been the lucky ones. The mountain may once again be off-limits to anyone other than the Turkish military forces safeguarding its border. Its geographical location may necessitate much tighter regulations for issuance of permits or none at all. The Turkish government cannot be expected to guarantee the safety of Mount Ararat exploration. The mountain is too large, 500 square miles, and the logistics and expense would be a burden when resources are at a premium. Russia is on the north, Iran to the east, and Iraq to the south. They have their hands full just patrolling their borders. The risks continue to escalate week by week. Even with the short optimum times for climbing and searching in July and August, why risk an international incident? The Turkish officials must weigh all the options both predictable and unpredictable.

Serious Ark researchers fully realize the danger and risks. They are literally placing their lives on the line. Will it be an avalanche, a rockslide, lightning, freezing, a broken leg, a twisted ankle, an attack by the ferocious Kurdish sheep dogs, cave bears, the deadly viper, a robbery by bandits, or an organized terrorist group which will unexpectedly end the search for any individual or group? Even death and being held hostage are not imagined possibilities. All these dangers have occurred to dedicated American explorers. We all seem to have the same missionary-type zeal, in spite of all obstacles, that the importance of the Ark's authentication outweighs personal safety and comfort.

Many factors have influence why the Ark's existence hasn't been physically verified. A bibliography of suggested publications has been listed for those who want this information and background in Ark research. A finger points toward a group of mountain people who are protecting the Ark from exploitation and defilement. Photographers are not to be encouraged. Mount Ararat is to the Armenians like the wailing wall is to the Jews. The Kurds are a unique group unto themselves. They want their own identity and autonomy. It is estimated that some 10 million Kurds inhabit a 74,000 square-mile territory within the borders of Turkey, Iran, Iraq, Syria and the Soviet Union. In Turkey alone there are an estimated six million Kurds. A political policy of assimilation exists in spite of the 1920 Treaty of Sevres which would have provided an autonomous Kurdish state within Turkey. God apparently has been using these Kurds to accomplish His divine will also.

God is still in control and it really makes little difference what well-meaning efforts are expended; if it is not in God's timetable, the status quo will continue. Does God use humans to accomplish His purpose?

Of course, the answer is, yes. Is it possible that God will use Ed's story some 42 years later for new clues and information to the world of the Ark's location and begin the final chapter before Jesus returns?

Chapter 11
In Conclusion

And it came to pass in the days of Noah, even so shall it be also in the days of the Son of Man. They ate, they drank, they married, they were given in marriage, until the day that Noah entered into the Ark, and the flood came, and destroyed them *all*. (Luke 17:26-27)

Was the flood a local phenomenon or a worldwide deluge? The above scripture, God's written word, is very clear in its answer that *"the flood came and destroyed them all."* Not a few, not a part, but *all* its inhabitants. Some can accept a local flood occurrence, but a worldwide catastrophe, never. If the flood was a local, select geographical event, then why any need for an ark? Noah spent some 120 years in its construction which provided ample time for God to have led him to an area of the earth that would have been danger-free. This would hold for all the beasts, birds, reptiles, et cetera.

What if this passage held another meaning, another insight? What if it were a sign that would signal the end of our present age and the imminent return of the Messiah? Noah had found favor in the eyes of God and the Ark was the method used to provide a safety vehicle. It was a way of escape from God's impending punishment. Noah had preached repentance and a turning away from man's ungodly ways. Nobody listened and no one took him seriously. Crazy Noah was a number one candidate for the "funny farm!" The time arrived when *"The Lord shut him in;"* God closed the door and the way of escape no longer existed. Jesus Christ is our Ark today. "I am the Way, the Truth and the Life. No man cometh unto the Father but by me." (John 14:6) Eternal life is still available. The door is still open, but the time will come when God will shut the door again. It will be shut in one of two ways, either by an individual's death or His return to planet Earth. I'm quite certain that there can be found finger marks, clawing up the Ark's side as a grim reminder of those individuals trying to get on board as the flood water rose higher and higher.

What if God will use the re-discovery, the physical proof of the Ark's reality as the last sign to unbelievers of the need to get on board before God again shuts the door? Another last opportunity to see and to believe. I don't know if this is God's purpose or not. There are, however, several reasons why I feel this may be a distinct possibility. Noah would not need to construct the Ark the way he did of gopher wood, pitch it without and within, et cetera, for it to last only one year. Then to be placed on God's special mountain, Ararat, and buried in the ice and snow (deep-freezer) and the mountain to be formed by a volcano. Then to have all the conditions present for additional preservation where the original wood is replaced by stone (petrification) and not to have a purpose in revealing it again at His appointed time. With the right conditions available the Ark could be preserved indefinitely. The constant earthquakes of eastern Turkey, the tremendous volcanic blast to the northeast part of the mountain in 1840, the present day-by-day rockslides and avalanches as the mountain slowly collapses, any of which could have completely destroyed any structure on the mountain. The fact remains that it is still visible. It is still on the mountain. God still has a very real purpose for having protected it these thousands of years. I have no problem with this because our God, who created it all, can protect what He wants to protect for as long as He wants. I had originally believed that it would be found completely intact. This apparently is not the case. Even the broken piece possibly has some significance and purpose. It has survived. Dr. R. H. Brown, director of the Geoscience Research Institute stated that "wood could become petrified within a few years if it remained saturated with water that had percolated through a layer of volcanic ash." All the conditions for preservation have been and are present on Mount Ararat. A coincidence? No, a predetermined plan.

Mevlana, an early Turkish philosopher, died on Sunday, December 17, 1273 in Konya, Turkey. Known as the sultan of scholars both in the East and West, this great thinker had inscribed upon his sarcophagus the following ode:

When I die and you see my coffin on their shoulders, do not suppose that I carry the trouble of the world with me. Do not cry for me, do not say "what misfortune," or alas. The time to thus lament is when you fall into Satan's trap. When you see my corpse do not bewail the separation. My meeting, my finding begins then. When they put me in the grave do not say farewell. The grace is the curtain before heaven's gate.
You have seen the sunset, so watch it rise. Setting does not harm the sun or moon.
To you it seems that they set, but in fact it is rebirth. The grave seems like a prison, but in fact it releases the soul from prison.

What seed ever fell to the ground without growing? Why do you not believe that the seed of man will grow when it is sown? What bucket was ever lowered into a well that did not come out full?
Why should you weep when Joseph falls into the well?
If you closed your mouth on this side at death, open it on the other.
Because you are far from the noise and bustle, you are in a spaceless world. From: Onder, Mehmet, *The Museums of Turkey*, Turkiye Is Bankasi Publication. Printed by: Dogus Matbaasi, Ankara, 1983, pp. 212-213)

Mevlana considered death to be a rebirth, a type of graduation ceremony when he would be united with God. This ode written some 700 years ago has implications for the world today. Our spirits are eternal. The world tells us that there are two absolutes. These are taxes and death. But death is only the beginning of forever. Eternity is real. To the believer we are "joint heirs with Christ." If Noah were alive today, he would be urging you to "get on board."

In the spring of 1984, I was flying to Texas on a commercial jet airliner and began a conversation with a well-educated engineer in the next seat to mine. The subject came up about my search in eastern Turkey for the Ark of Noah. He looked straight at me and said this: "A man of your intelligence and archaeological background? You can't really believe in that Biblical story?" I answered, "Not only do I believe it, it is not a myth; the Ark was a real structure and there was a real Flood." It was very apparent he would not accept any scriptural references, so I began to relate other written accounts, sightings, documented historical references, and I shared just a few examples of the over 200 similar flood stories passed down from generation to generation by peoples in all five continents. After a few moments, the engineer got very quiet and turned to me and said, "If you people actually find the Ark, then I'll need to get my act together." How much more time? What additional evidence does the world need to "get its act together?"

I wish it weren't so difficult for even some Christians to believe. "Faith is the substance of things hoped for, the evidence of things not seen." (Hebrews 11:1) Some individuals just have to hold, touch and place the evidence under the scrutiny of an electron microscope before they can allow themselves to believe. Noah had none of the testimonies and evidence that we in the 20th Century have at our fingertips. Yet Noah believed and was saved.

In the preparation of this book I have had a very serious problem in deciding how many specific names and locations should be exposed.

There is no doubt in my mind from this information that, given the freedom to explore the mountain without exploration limitations, one can climb to the exact canyon in which the Ark of Noah still rests. The landmarks to retrace Ed's climb are available. What then happens? A tourist invasion or closing down of the mountain to all visitors? Mt. Ararat is in a military zone and how will the thousands of requests be handled? Will this disrupt the Kurds living in the village in a positive or negative way? Will the Turkish government confiscate the artifacts from the Ark and place them in a museum in Ankara or Istanbul? There is some question as to whether the Turkish authorities are aware that artifacts exist. If they weren't before, they are now. My conclusion was to be specific. This new knowledge is too important, too significant to be retained by a select few. Will people start worshiping the objects and lose perspective of what the Ark of Noah and the Biblical Flood represent? I certainly hope not. No one group, denomination, or religion has an exclusive audience and rapport with our Creator. This information has implications and significance to the world, to the Christian, the Jew, the Gentile, the Moslem, and all others. The Turkish government has been very cooperative in allowing Americans access to the mountain. As one Turkish Moslem stated, "When the Ark of Noah is verified as really existing and its location known, it will bring peace to all the Mideast at least for a short period of time."

"And the Lord shut him in."

Chapter 12
Synopsis of Ed Davis's Story

1. Ed Davis viewed Noah's Ark sometime in July, 1943.
2. The Ark is located on the northeast side of Mount Ararat in the Kars province.
3. The Ark in 1943 was in two parts. The smaller section is resting some one-half mile from the main structure.
4. Somewhere between 100 and 200 feet was uncovered at this time.
5. All the wood within and without the Ark is petrified.
6. Wooden pegs, not metal spikes, were used in its construction and the larger beams have splices.
7. The Ark is pitched for preservation and a water-tight seal.
8. The one large door was still intact and was in a closed position. This door swings from the bottom outward.
9. The door is located on the Ark's left side facing the front end which was covered by ice, snow and rockslides and debris.

10. Some years the Ark is hidden completely and some years portions or the entire structure may be visible.

12. The Ark has three stories and the living compartments were at the middle, top section with a low superstructure and flat roof above.

13. Animal and bird cages were examined, both large and small. Feathers have been found inside some of these cages. The larger cages were located in the rear section, the section that was exposed in 1943.

14. Artifacts have been recovered from the Ark. These include: pitch, cage doors, latches, pottery jars and bowls, honey, beans, shepherd's staffs, oil lamps, and one metal hammer and wedge.

15. Water basins made from animal skins (stomachs) are located throughout the Ark's interior at all levels.

16. The bottom of the Ark has a large bottom ridge (beam) and the sides are slightly rounded from its base to the top outside walls which join the flat top decking.

17. The Ark is very sacred to the Kurds who are guarding it from outsiders, especially non-Moslems.

18. There is no firepit on the Ark. Oil stoves were probably used to cook and for heat. Oil lamps were used for lights.

19. Ed Davis passed Jacob's Well and the Moslem shrine located near Ahora Village.

20. Ed was taken to the Ark. He did not search for it.

21. Abas-Abas was educated for a short time at a Presbyterian school in Teheran, Iran. He spoke broken English, German and French.

22. Abas-Abas gave Ed Davis pictures of his village and the camp where the horses were mounted.

23. Doomsday Point drops into the Ahora Gorge.

24. Caves were slept in every night while the group was on Mount Ararat.

25. Old writing, inscriptions and paintings were found on every cave wall.

26. Photographs have been taken of the Ark. The author is following up on these new leads provided by Mr. Davis.

27. Cameras and photography of the Ark are discouraged and forbidden by the Kurds. Even the photographs are sacred and holy to those carefully guarding the Ark's location.

28. Ed Davis has the stone knife he found in one of the caves on the mountain.

29. Ed has a record of his trip written in his personal Bible.

30. Ed Davis may very well be the first American to view Noah's Ark even though there have been reports of four sightings in the 1941-1945 time period. Unfortunately there are no set dates for any of these four

sightings, and they are still questionable due to lack of verifiable information.

32. The reason Ed Davis was adopted by the Kurdish family of Abas-Abas cannot be revealed until after his death. This request was made by Ed Davis, and the author will honor what was shared.

34. The Ark was resting on its right side in July of 1943.

35. There are forty-eight compartments within the Ark's living quarters.

Chapter 13
Some Personal History of Ed Davis

Ed Davis was born July 11, 1905 on a work train between Texas and Oklahoma. Living on a ranch near Wichita, Texas, he learned to brand, shoe horses, and do all the many duties required to exist in the early American southwest. Ed was older than most when he enlisted in the Army at Santa Fe, New Mexico on January 24, 1942 and was discharged from the service on September 23, 1945 at Ft. Bliss, Texas. He married Pauline just before his enlistment. No children were born from this union. He was assigned to the 363rd Army Corps of Engineers, Company E and was sent to Hamadan, Iran. On December 28, 1944 he was transferred to the 334th Engineers and was flown to Europe to fight the Germans until the end of World War II. Ed was awarded four battle stars, one bronze star and one silver star for his participation in the defeat of America's enemies.

Following his discharge he was employed by the Bandelier National Monument near Los Alamos for four years and at Sandia Base as an inspector for 20 years. Since his retirement, he and Pauline have raised goats on their acreage in the south valley of Albuquerque, New Mexico. Their Nubian goats have been national champions for some fourteen successive years.

Ed made his own saddle and is a true artist with leather. There are not many things that Ed Davis has missed in his eighty years of adventure. The day he had to play mid-wife and help a baby girl enter this world is a classic example of being in the right place at the wrong time. Ed will be the first to tell you that his climb up Mount Ararat and actually looking upon Noah's Ark has to be the greatest thrill and privilege any human could ever experience. "Why me," he often asks himself. "I don't understand it, but I'm very thankful it really happened. Our God is so very, very good. Someday I sincerely hope the entire world can see what I saw. The Ark is very real."

Chapter 14
The Missing Russian Photographs of Noah's Ark

In the summer of 1970 Dave GuMaer, while on a speaking tour in Oklahoma City for the American Opinion's speakers bureau, met an elderly Russian gentleman, Mr. Aramais Arutunoff. Dave had been giving a series of lectures on the world communist conspiracy starting with the Russian revolution of 1917. This Russian man came up to him after his speech and made some very cryptic remarks about the fact that he had been living in Russia at that time, and he would like to fill Dave in on the names, dates, places and key players in the revolution. Dave's assignments had been concluded, and since he was an investigative reporter, he would take Arutunoff up on his offer to meet together. The following day Dave met with Mr. Arutunoff in Bartlesville only to find that Mr. Arutunoff was the owner of a very large oil company and a very wealthy individual. The ensuing conversation showed Dave that Mr. Arutunoff was not only a very knowledgeable and intelligent individual, but a man with a photographic memory. For the next two days he listened with awe and amazement as this individual outlined his personal experiences in Russia during that period of the revolution. He explained to Dave facts concerning the world-wide communist conspiracy of which he wasn't aware at that time. What he told Dave essentially was this:

Back in 1917 as a youth in St. Petersburg, the city which Peter the Great built, he (Arutunoff) watched and observed the massive build-up of the Bolshevik communits working toward the overthrow of the Czar of Russia. (Czar Nicholas) He said that these individuals were extremely subversive, and their goal was to undermine and destroy the government of the Czar. He was very much concerned over the fact that his own brother Ananias was a Bolshevik and that he had been actively working with Lenin toward the eventual overthrow of the Czar and the Russian government. Czar Nicholas was a Christian, and at that time Russia was one of the largest Christian nations in the world. This was one of the major reasons the communists wanted power to destroy his country. Christianity and communism are incompatible.

During this period of time Arutunoff had been working in the Russian oil fields, and he was very much against what the communists were doing. He realized that he must escape from Russia with his family into Berlin, which he accomplished. While in Berlin, he attempted to raise some funds and obtain a patent on a revolutionary drill-bit which he had invented. This invention would increase oil field productivity. Arutunoff was turned down at evey bank, not because he didn't have a great invention, but because he was not a communist. Had he been a communist he would have obtained instant funding.

After his sojourn in Berlin, Arutunoff left for the United States, arriving in New York City. Again he began an intensified effort to obtain funding for his oil-bit project and to protect his invention with a patent. He was again turned down. Some years later he eventually ended up in Oklahoma working in the oil fields. It was in Oklahoma that he finally received his patent and the funding to begin production. Because of this, Arutunoff became very wealthy and became the sole owner of his own oil company.

He then continued to tell Dave about events, names, and places that you rarely read about in history concerning the Russian revolution. Arutunoff said the revolution was financed by the United States, England, and by international banking groups who apparently wanted the Bolsheviks to take over control from the Czar. This group had financed Lenin with twenty million dollars in gold to help accomplish this purpose. Arutunoff emphasized that it was not the masses who rose in opposition to the Czar but the opposition was instead led by a handful of highly-trained, educated communists, many of whom had been trained in foreign countries for their assignment in Russia.

Shortly before the overthrow of the government, the Czar had commissioned some one hundred White Russian soldiers to undertake an investigative trip to Mount Ararat in search of the fabled Ark of Noah that was described in Genesis. This group of soldiers made their trek up the Russian side of Mount Ararat and after much difficulty reached a point on the mountain where the Ark was said to be buried under ice and snow. This was exactly what they found: a petrified barge extending from beneath an ice peak. The Ark of Noah was real and was located on Mount Ararat.

Mr. Arutunoff said that some years later he met a Russian soldier, one of the survivors of this expedition, who informed him in great detail of what they had seen, the measurements of the boat, the photographs which had been taken, along with many other facts and details concerning the expedition. This soldier described the surveyors, photographers, artists and scientists who were on the mountain specifically to find the Ark and to prove that it existed on Mount Ararat. They did prove this fact. From what Dave GuMaer could remember from Arutunoff's description, the dimensions of the Ark were some 450 feet long, by fifty feet high, by some 100 to 150 feet wide. It was in the shape of a barge. The Ark had a narrow catwalk running along the top length of the barge. The soldiers had walked inside the structure and had observed animal stalls of all different sizes made of wood. All the wood was petrified. They also found edible wheat and honey. The soldiers chipped away pieces of the petrified wood for later analysis to determine what type of trees were used in its construction.

It was at this point when Mr. Arutunoff reached into a drawer in his desk and very casually removed two photographs which he laid in front of Dave GuMaer. Here were the photographs of Noah's Ark taken by the Russian photographer on Mount Ararat. Dave remembers them as being grainy and enlarged but clearly showing the barge Arutunoff had just described. The pictures were of a large, barge-type craft protruding from the ice. The barge was on a shelf overhanging a frozen lake below. About three-fourths of the structure was still encased in an ice pack. The Ark was tilted at an angle. In the doorway of the Ark stood three Russian soldiers linked arm in arm. The doorway appeared to be about twenty-five feet high and some twenty-five or thirty feet wide. Off to one side of the Ark was some type of wooden altar.

Arutunoff then continued his story of the expedition. These Russian soldiers were on direct orders from the Czar to measure, photograph and survey everything they found. After this was completed, their samples taken, and their sketches carefully catalogued, the soldiers proceeded to leave the site on Mount Ararat and return with all this important data and immediately report to the Czar. By the time they returned, the Russian revolution was in full operation. The Russian army was running rampant throughout the country. All but two of the soldiers involved in the Ark expedition were captured and arrested by the Bolsheviks and then executed. Anything which gives support or credence to the Bible must be destroyed by any communist. Of the two that escaped, one was the surveyor and the other soldier was the photographer. The surveyor apparently stayed somewhere in Europe while the photographer made his way to the United States. He would be safer here in America. It was some years later that Mr. Arutunoff made the acquaintance of this Russian photographer and was given copies of the Ark pictures. These were the very same photographs Dave GuMaer was shown. (See sketch page 49.)

Where are the photographs now? After the death of Mr. Arutunoff, most of his personal papers have been stored by family members. His immediate family have no recollection of their father ever showing them the two photographs. Why? Was Mr. Arutunoff worried about some possible future problems these photographs might cause his family? Why would Mr. Arutunoff show Dave GuMaer, a total stranger, these important photographs? The reader can draw his own conclusions and suppositions.

Violet Cummings comments on all of the mysterious disappearances of verifiable data in her book *Noah's Ark: Fact or Fable* that "for years it had been increasingly obvious that some power beyond human ken must be at work to counteract or completely destroy every shred of concrete proof for the existence of the Ark."

Eryl Cummings and this author have received permission to search Mr. Arutunoff's papers. Hopefully somewhere hidden in some forgotten file or trunk these missing photographs may be found. Clue by clue, story by story, fact by fact, the reality of Noah's Ark is being confirmed to a doubting world.

The reader must now realize the importance of Ed Davis's story in relation to all the dead-end searches which previously have faced the serious Ark researchers.

Suggested Reading

Violet Cummings, *Noah's Ark: Fact or Fable?* (San Diego: Creation-Science Research Center, 1972)

Violet M. Cummings, *Has Anybody Really Seen Noah's Ark?* (Creation-Life Publishers, 1982)

James B. Irwin with Monte Unger, *More Than An Ark On Ararat* (Broadman Press, 1985)

John D. Morris, *Adventure on Ararat* (Creation-Life Publishers, 1973)

John Warwick Montgomery, *The Quest for Noah's Ark* (Minneapolis, Minnesota: Bethany Fellowship, Inc., 1972)

Fernand Navarra, *Noah's Ark: I Touched It* (Logos International, 1974)

Donald W. Patten, *The Biblical Flood and the Ice Epoch* (Pacific Meridian Publishing Co., 1966)

Alfred M. Rehwinkel, *The Flood in the Light of the Bible, Geology, and Archaeology* (Concordia Publishing House, 1951)

John C. Whitcomb, Jr., and Henry M. Morris, *The Genesis Flood* (Baker Book House, 1961)

Sketch of the Russian photograph of Noah's Ark which Dave GuMaer observed at Bartlesville, Oklahoma in 1970.

Ed Davis as he looked in 1943 in Hamadan, Iran. Ed has the distinguished honor of having been the first American to view Noah's Ark.

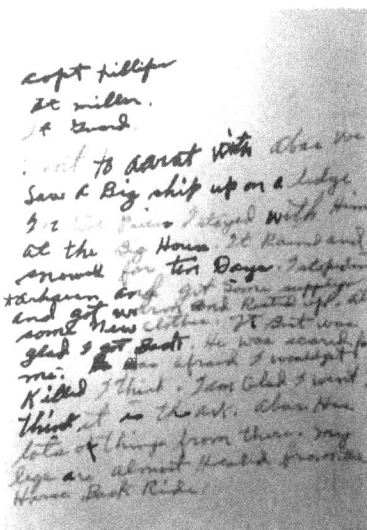

Ed Davis's handwritten account of his eighteen-day trip up Mount Ararat and his sighting of Noah's Ark. This was written in his Bible immediately following his return to Tehran, Iran in 1943.

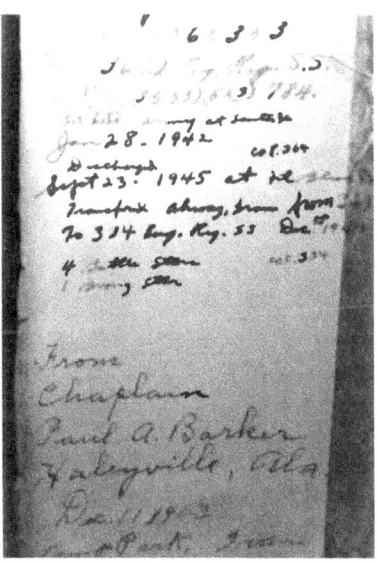

Photograph of Ed Davis's Bible listing personal information and dates.

Mount Ararat viewed from the Iranian side.

Kurdish village where Ed Davis began his climb at the base of Mount Ararat.

Street scene of the village of Abas-Abas in 1943.

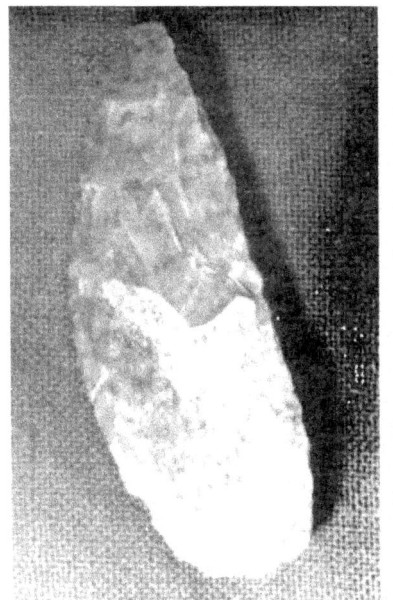
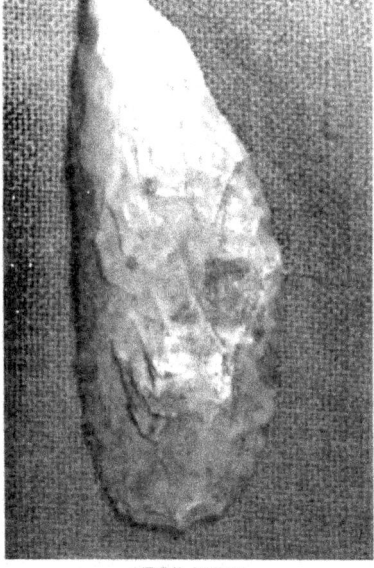

BOTTOM VIEW　　　　　　　　**TOP VIEW**

Stone tool (combination knife and scraper) found in a cave on Mount Ararat by Ed Davis. 75 mm. long, 30 mm. wide, weight 23.3 grams, brownish tan chert, age unknown.

Iranian salt mine near Mount Ararat.

Fossil shells near Mount Ararat giving evidence of the Flood.

Photo given Ed Davis by Abas-Abas showing how difficult the trail up Mount Ararat can be when covered with snow and frozen ice. What year the photograph was taken in unknown.

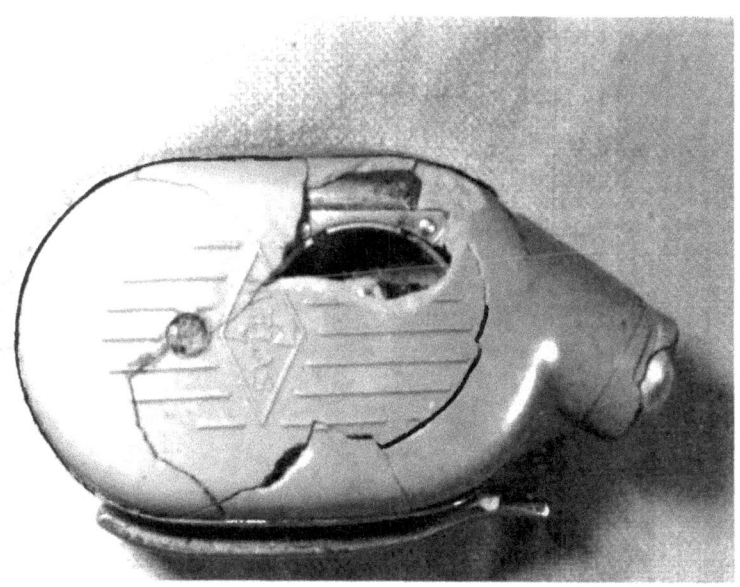

Flashlight given Ed Davis by Abas-Abas and used for signaling on Mount Ararat.

Left: Hadji Mirza Shahrastany, relative of Avatollah Khomenini. Right: the father of Ayatollah Khomenini's cousin. Ed Davis had several conversations with this man while in Iran.

Ayatollah Khomenini's cousin and Ed Davis in Tehran, 1943. Notice the family resemblance. Khomenini's cousin left, Ed Davis center, unidentified soldier right.

The Shah of Iran during World War II. Ed Davis became close friend and hunting partner of George, the Shah's brother.

The first queen of the Shah of Iran, King Farouk's sister. She gave Ed Davis a pair of her earrings (above right) in 1943 for helping correct a hoof problem with one of her favorite horses. The earrings, which she removed from her ears to give to him, were gold and red carnelian.

The Shah and his wife greeting guests in Tehran in 1943. Ed Davis was a guest of the royal family at the palace on several occasions.

Interior photograph of the palace of the Shah of Iran which Ed Davis was invited to visit in Tehran.

The Shah of Iran's throne in 1943.

Stalin, Roosevelt and Churchill at Tehran, Iran, November, 1943. The theme of the conference was to prepare for the D-Day invasion of World War II. This was the pre-Yalta Conference. Stalin had intelligence information that the Germans were going to make a raid on the conference and kill them all. It did not happen but they were prepared for such an attack by German paratroopers.

President Franklin D. Roosevelt reviewing American troops stationed in Tehran, Iran, 1943.

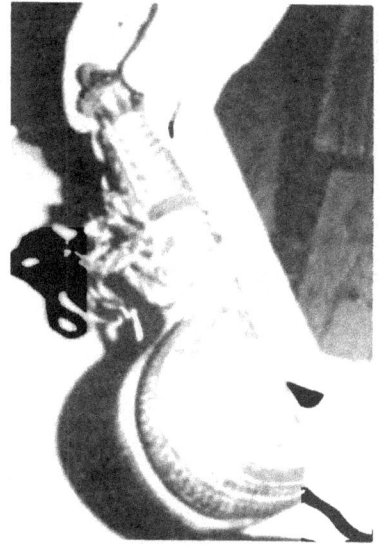

Silver dagger with Damascus steel blade given to Ed Davis by the Shah of Iran's brother, George. the blade had been tempered in blood.

Hand-tooled leather canteen given to Ed Davis by Abas-Abas and used by his Kurdish family regularly until 1917 when metal canteens became available.

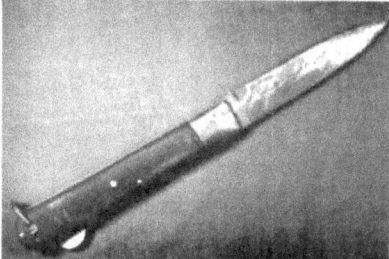

Knife Ed Davis used on his Mount Ararat trip.

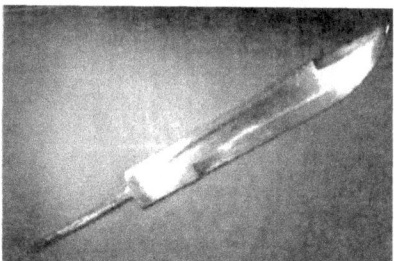

Knife given Ed Davis by his close Kurdish friend. He used this knife to cut roasted goat and sheep meat during his stay in Iran.

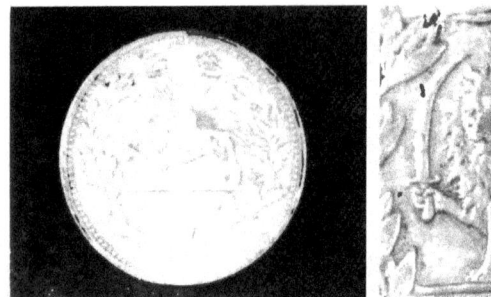 

Modern Iranian silver coin collected by Ed Davis while in Hamadan, Iran, 1943. An enlargement of the lion and saber is shown on the right.

Ancient Persian coins uncovered by Ed Davis during road excavations in Iran.

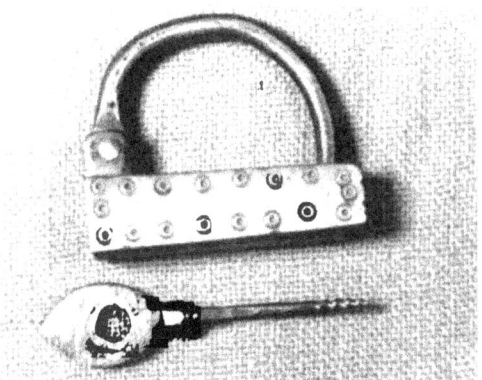

An Iranian lock and key from Ed Davis's collection of Iranian artifacts. Notice the unique key for unlocking the mechanism.

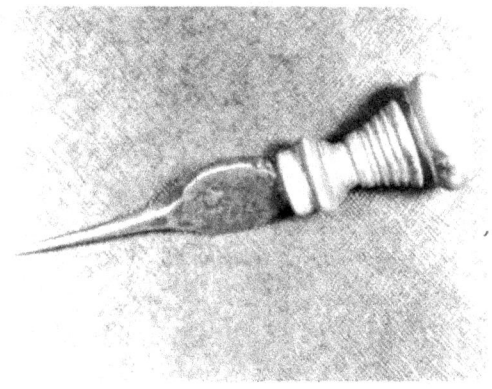

This metal awl was given Ed Davis by a Kurdish craftsman and is entirely handmade.

Left: Large carved pipe given Ed Davis by an old Kurdish historian and story-teller. Right: Iranian rubies from the collection of Ed Davis. Even when photographed in black and white, the faceting reflects a sparkling beauty.

Lonely apple tree located in the traditional location of the Biblical Garden of Eden in Iran which Ed Davis visited.

One of Ed Davis's favorite photographs is of a painting depicting an old Kurdish story teller. Legends and historical accounts are still passed from generation to generation by the village historian.

Ed Davis and old Kurdish gentleman swapping stories near Hamadan, Iran, 1943.

Ed Davis shown directing road construction near Hamadan, Iran.

American G.I.'s at the tunnel entrance into Russia from Iran.

Ed Davis and G.I. friend examining Persian bas-reliefs south of Tehran near Persepolis.

Another series of bas-relief carvings depicting ancient life in Persia which Ed Davis visited in 1943.

It was in Iran that Ed Davis met his first Persian princess. This princess had fifteen eunuchs to serve her every wish and command. None of the eunuchs was under six feet eight inches tall.

Ed Davis had an opportunity to visit this Persian harem during his military career in Iran. Notice the women with their hands on their heads are slaves.

Kurdish bakery where Ed Davis would occasionally buy fresh baked bread.

A typical Kurdish meat market located in a village north of Hamadan, Iran. Goat shish kebab, according to Ed Davis, can be delicious when cooked properly.

Metal locks hang from slits in the skin of this Iranian holy man.

Many products can be manufactured from the wool of sheep and goats. This Kurdish camp visited by Ed Davis had a very large flock. Villagers roasted a goat in honor of their guest.

Chi, a hot tea, is offered to all who visit this remote Kurdish camp in northern Iran. Foreign visitors were not common in 1943. Ed Davis enjoyed teasing these children.

Above: Wooden plow used by Kurdish villagers near Hamadan, Iran. Below: Ed Davis shown trying his farming skill with a wooden plow near Hamadan, Iran.

Left: Ed Davis always enjoyed every opportunity to take a ride in an Iranian taxi. At least you didn't need to worry about flat tires and a dead battery.

Right: A Kurdish farmer Ed Davis met near Hamadan, Iran. Everybody likes to have his picture taken.

Grass must be carefully harvested in the fall of each year to feed the animals during the cold winter months in Iran. Ed Davis spent many weekends visiting remote Kurdish villages during his service career in Iran.

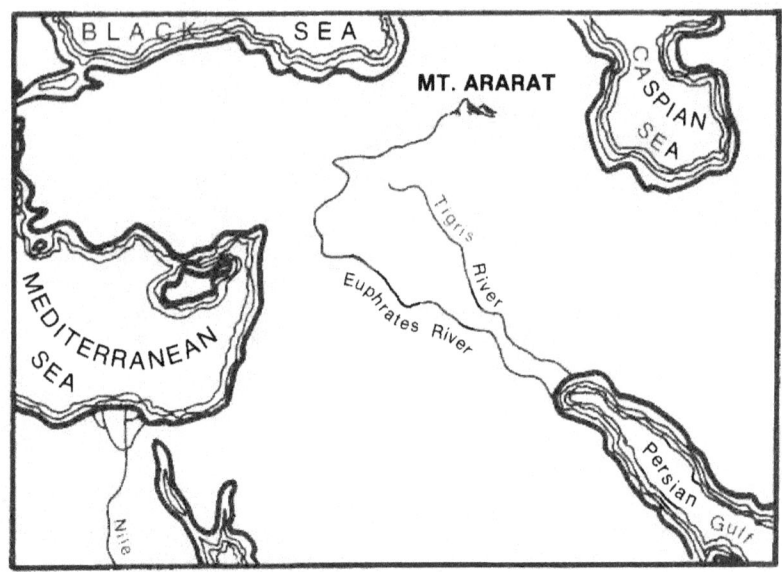

Drawing showing the beginnings of the Tigris and Euphrates rivers ending in the Persian Gulf.

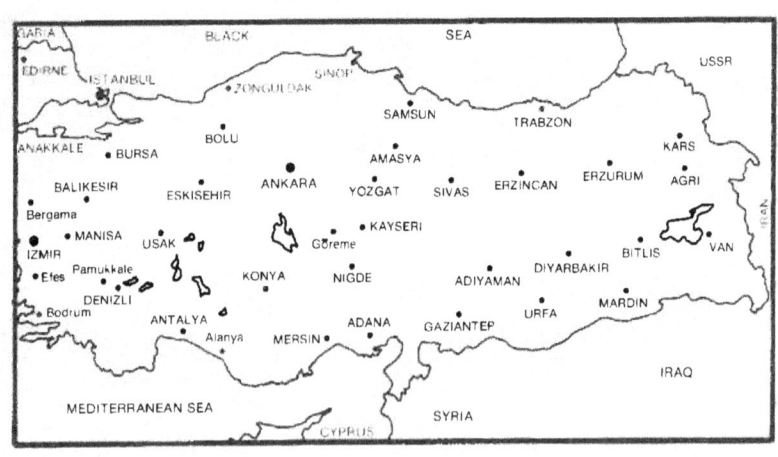

Map of Turkey.

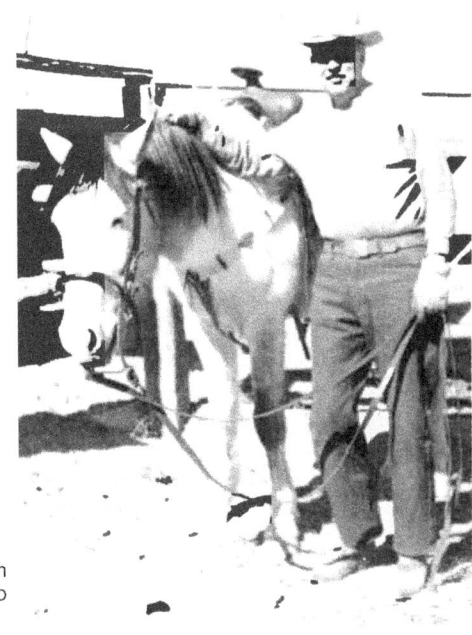

Ed Davis taking a break from branding cattle on the Rio Puerco Ranch in 1982.

Ed Davis and Dr. Don Shockey on January 5, 1986.

Horseback riding is still one of Ed's favorite ways to relax.

Ed Davis adjusting his 65-year-old elk-hide chaps.

The next series of photographs taken on Mount Ararat is included to differentiate from those connected with the Ed Davis story and to give the reader additional pictorial information about more recent expeditions on Mount Ararat in search of Noah's Ark.

The Kurdish village of Dogubayazit was the last stop before beginning the 1984 expedition's climb up the south slope of Mount Ararat in our search for the Ark. It is here that final clearance and permission must be obtained from local Agri officials.

The date 1782 was carved into this tombstone in an old Kurdish cemetery near Igdir, Turkey. Sculptured animal head motifs are seen throughout this ancient cemetery. Igdir is another Kurdish village located on the north side of Mount Ararat.

It was here at Eli that the author began his 1984 search for the Ark. Vehicles must stop at this location and can go no farther. All climbing gear is loaded on the backs of the long-legged Kurdish horses. Horses were used for two days and then all supplies had to be carried in back-packs.

An old Kurdish proverb states that "the Kurds have no friends." The Kurds have no central government of their own and live mostly in inaccessible mountain areas. Without the expert help of our Kurdish friends both in mountaineering and horsemanship, the 1984 expedition would have been even more difficult.

The author following the Kurdish horsemen along the trail toward the south slope of Mount Ararat during the first day of hiking in 1984.

Finding a rock-free, level plot of ground to erect a tent can be frustrating. The 1984 expedition appreciated this area, complete with a small stream of water nearby. It was here that Kurdish natives showed us many of their rugs and handcrafts, hoping we would buy them.

Rest stops are a welcome relief to both the pack horses and climbers. After hiking for four hours from our starting point at Eli, the mountain seems just as far away as when we began.

The steep, rock strewn slopes of Mount Ararat make climbing very slow and difficult, even at the mountain's lower elevations.

Drinking water is always a problem on Mount Ararat. It was here on the mountain that our canteens were filled and denatured iodine added to protect the climbers from intestinal parasites.

Hogback ridge on Mount Ararat. The mountain is subjected to continual rockslides and avalanches. Dislodged rocks are a constant danger faced by climbers. For safety reasons, overnight camps are situated on ridges away from potential hazards whenever possible. Notice the tent in the lower foreground.

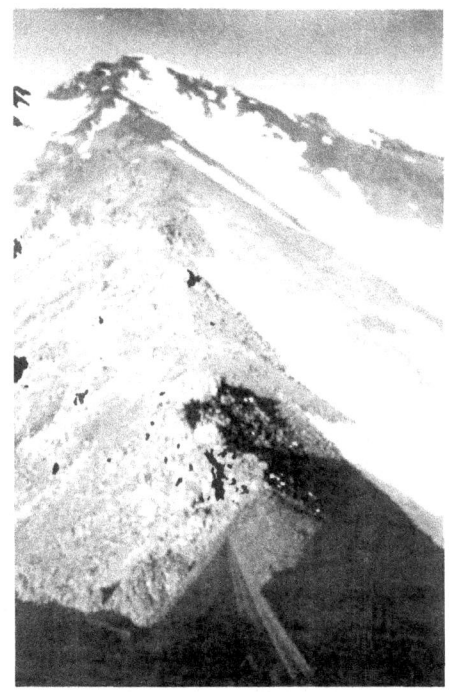

When the fog arrives there is nothing more to do than wait. Climbers have been lost and separated from their group by not following basic mountaineering rules. Proper equipment is a major requirement for survival on Mount Ararat. Three feet of snow can fall within a few hours. Freezing rain can numb the senses. Northface equipment was used by the author and it can be highly recommended.

Icicles on the rocks near Camp Three. The porous volcanic rocks and turf immediately absorb the melting ice and snow as the temperature rises above the freezing mark.

Notice the large boulders which have rolled off the rocky ridges onto the snow and ice field. Sometimes crossing these areas can not be avoided.

Dr. Jim Davies is seen beginning his careful hike across the snow field. Hidden snow-filled fissures and crevasses are tested constantly with the climber's ice axe and climbing poles. A twenty-two-square-mile ice-cap covers the top of Mount Ararat.

Parrot glacier can be seen in the distance snaking its "S" shaped path down the west side of Mount Ararat.

Parrot glacier was named for Dr. Frederick Parrot, who in 1829 climbed to the summit of Mount Ararat. American search teams originally concentrated their exploration in this area of the mountain.

It was at this location that Fernand Navarra probed into this milk-white lake at the base of the Parrot glacier and recovered small pieces of black, water-logged wood. Additional wood fragments have been found around this pond during later searches.

The mountain is very deceiving. One moment the sunshine is warming the slopes and the next moment you can not see ten feet in any direction due to the thick blanket of clouds and fog which engulfs the climber. When the fog moves in, all activities stop. It is very easy to become disoriented in such conditions.

Ahora Gorge was created by a gigantic volcanic explosion in 1840. Located on the northeast side of Mount Ararat near the Russian-Iranian border, the old Kurdish village of Ahora has been a starting point for search teams. Recently this area of Mount Ararat has been closed to all expeditions.

The rugged, hidden canyons and ravines located at the upper region of Ahora Gorge are a climber's nemesis. It is in this general area of Mount Ararat that Noah's Ark is believed to be located.

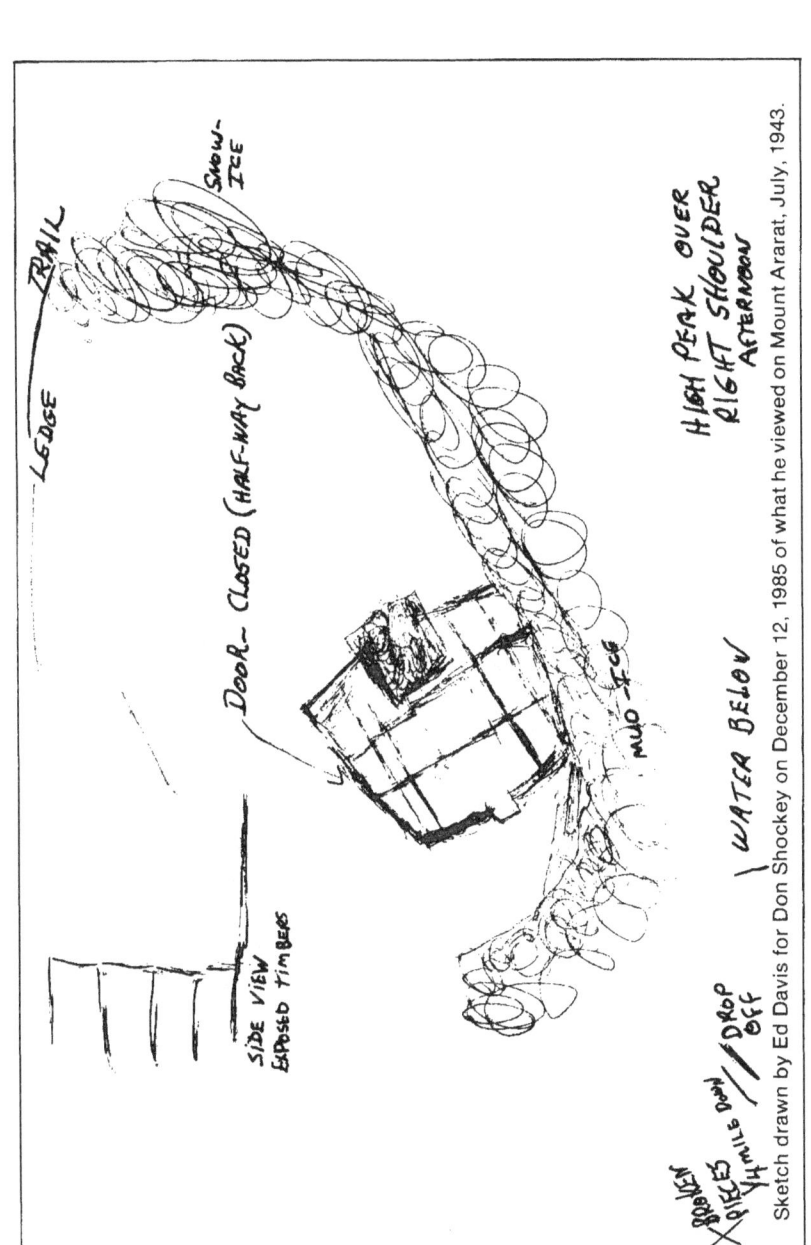

Sketch drawn by Ed Davis for Don Shockey on December 12, 1985 of what he viewed on Mount Ararat, July, 1943.

33, Pont Street,
S.W.

2 Dec. 1909

Messrs Longmans Green & Co.
39 Paternoster Row
E.C.

Dear Sirs,

With reference to the application made by Messrs Alphonse Picard & Sils to reproduce 4 plates from my "Armenia" in their "Manuel d'art Byzantin", will you kindly inform them that I have no objection to this, provided that at the end of each title, both in the body of the book and in the index, they state that the illustration is "reproduced from Mr Lynch's Armenia" and provided that they would have the courtesy to send me a copy of the publication free of charge.

Yours faithfully,

H.F.B. Lynch

WSg.

Letter owned by Dr. Don Shockey from Henry Finnis B. Lynch (1862-1913). Lynch instituted new trade routes into Persia. He journeyed through the Caucasus, Armenia in 1893-94, reaching the summit of Mount Ararat in September 1893. The letter is in regard to a publisher's wanting permission to reproduce four of his plates previously printed in "Manuel d'Art Byzantin."

Part 2

A Look at Genesis and Science

By
Dr. Walter Brown

This is a brief summary of 116 categories of scientific evidence that support a sudden creation and oppose gradual evolution. Evidences 1-36 relate to the life sciences, 37-87 relate to the astronomical sciences, and 88-116 relate to the earth sciences.

This information is generally being withheld from students. If this evidence were not censored from the public classroom but openly presented, better science education would result.

Notes are keyed under the appropriate evidence number in the Notes and Reference section following.

EVOLUTION* HAS NEVER BEEN OBSERVED

1. Spontaneous generation (the emergence of life from non-living matter) has never been observed. All observations have shown that life only comes from life. This has been so consistently observed that it is called the Law of Biogenesis. The theory of evolution conflicts with this law by claiming that life came from non-living matter.

2. Mendel's laws of genetics explain almost all of the physical variations that are observed within life, such as in the dog family. A logical consequence of these laws and their modern day refinements is that there are *limits* to such variation. (a,b) Breeding experiments have also confirmed that these boundaries exist. (c-f)

3. Acquired characteristics cannot be inherited. (a)

4. Natural selection cannot produce *new* genes; it only *selects* among preexisting characteristics.

5. Mutations are the only proposed mechanism by which new genetic material becomes available for evolution. (a,b) Rarely, if ever, is a mutation beneficial to an organism in its natural environment. Almost all (perhaps all) observable mutations are harmful (c,e); many are lethal. (f-h)

6. No known mutation has ever produced a form of life having both greater complexity and greater viability than any of its ancestors. (a-e)

7. Over seventy years (a) of fruit-fly experiments, involving 2,700 consecutive generations, give absolutely no basis for believing that any natural or artificial process can cause an increase in complexity and viability. No clear genetic improvement has ever been observed despite the many unnatural efforts to increase mutation rates. (b-f)

8. There is no reason to believe that mutations could ever produce any new organs such as the eye (a), the ear, or the brain. (b,c) Just the human heart, a ten-ounce pump that will operate without maintenance or lubrication for about 75 years, is an engineering marvel. (d)

9. There is no direct evidence that any major group of animals or

---

*By *evolution* we mean a naturally occurring, beneficial change that produces *increasing complexity*. When referring to the evolution of life, this increasing complexity would be shown if the offspring of one form of life had a different, improved, and reproducible set of vital organs that its ancestors did not have. This is sometimes called organic evolution, the molecules-to-man theory, or *macro*evolution. *Micro*-evolution, on the other hand, does not involve increasing complexity. It only involves changes in shapes, colors, sizes, or minor chemical alterations—changes that both creationists and evolutionists agree are relatively trivial and easily observed. It is macroevolution, then, which requires increasing complexity, that is being to hotly contested today, and this is what we will mean by the term evolution.

plants arose from any other major group. (a-c) The hypothetical evolutionary tree has no branches. (d)

10. All species appear perfectly developed, not half-developed. They show design. (a) There are no examples of half-developed feathers, eyes (b), skin, tubes (arteries, veins, intestines, etc.), or any of thousands of other vital organs. For example, if a limb were to evolve into a wing, it would become a bad limb long before it became a good wing.

11. No verified form of extraterrestrial life of any kind has ever been observed. If evolution occurred on earth, one would expect that at least simple forms of life, such as microbes, would have been found by the elaborate experiments sent to the moon and Mars.

12. If languages evolved, the earliest languages should be the simplest. On the contrary, language studies reveal that the more ancient the language (for example, Latin, 200 B.C.; Greek, 800 B.C.; and Vedic Sanskrit, 1500 B.C.), the more complex it is with respect to syntax, cases, genders, moods, voices, tenses, and verb forms. The best evidence indicates that languages *devolve*. (a-c)

13. Studies of the thirty-six documented cases of children who were raised without contact with other humans (feral children) show that human speech appears to be learned only from other humans. Apparently, humans do not automatically speak. If so, the first humans must have been endowed with a speaking ability. There is no evidence that language has evolved. (a)

14. Codes are apparently produced only by intelligence, not natural processes or chance. A code is a set of rules for converting information from one useful form to another. Examples of coded information include: ideas coded by alphabetical letters on a printed page or by signals transmitted electrically; music coded in indentations on a phonographic record or by magnetic patterns on a magnetic tape.

The genetic material that controls the physical processes in life is coded information. It also is accompanied by elaborate transmission and duplication systems, without which the genetic material would be useless and life would cease. Therefore, it is most reasonable that this genetic code, the accompanying transmission and duplication systems, and all living organisms, which without exception rely on this code, were produced by high intelligence using NONnatural or SUPERnatural processes.

Likewise, no natural process has ever been observed to produce a *program*. A program is a planned sequence of steps to accomplish some goal. Computer programs are common examples. The information stored on the genetic material of all living organisms is a complex program. Since programs are not produced by chance or natural processes, some intelligent, SUPERnatural source probably developed these programs.

THE ARGUMENTS FOR EVOLUTION ARE OUTDATED AND OFTEN ILLOGICAL

15. It is illogical to maintain that similarities between different forms of life always imply a common ancestor (a); they may imply a common designer. In fact, in the cases where experiments have demonstrated that similar structures are controlled by different genes (b,c), a common designer is the more likely explanation.

16. The existence of human organs whose function is unkown does not imply that they are vestiges of organs from our evolutionary ancestors. In fact, as medical knowledge has increased, the functions of all of these organs have been discovered. (a) The widespread absence of vestigial organs implies that evolution never happened.

17. There are many single-cell forms of life, but there are no forms of animal life with 2, 3, 4, . . . , or even 20 cells. (a,b) If organic evolution happened, these forms of life should exist in great abundance. None do. The evolutionary tree has no trunk. (c)

18. As an embryo develops, it does not pass through the adult stages of its alleged evolutionary ancestors. Embryologists no longer consider the superficial similarities that exist between a few embryos and the adult forms of simpler animals as evidence for evolution. (a-h) The drawings by Ernst Haeckel, which led to this widespread belief, were deliberately falsified. (i-m)

19. Stories claiming that primitive, ape-like men have been found are overstated. (a-c) Piltdown man is now an acknowledged hoax, and yet it was in the textbooks for over forty years. (d) The fragmentary evidence for Nebraska man turned out to be a pig's tooth. Prior to 1978, the known remains of Ramapithecus consisted merely of a handful of teeth and jaw fragments. It is now known that these fragments were pieced together incorrectly by Louis Leakey (e) so as to resemble portions of the human jaw. (f) Ramapithecus was just an ape. (g) The discoverer of Java man later acknowledged that Java man was similar to a large gibbon (h,i) and that he had withheld evidence to that effect. (j-m) Peking man is considered by many experts to be the remains of apes that were systematically decapitated and exploited for food by true man. (n,o) Furthermore, Skull 1470, discovered by Richard Leakey, is more human-like and yet older than Java man, Peking man, and the Australopithecines. (p,q) Detailed computer studies of the Australopithecines, which were made famous by Louis and Mary Leakey, are

actually quite distinct from both man and apes. (r-t) Lucy, a type of Australopithecine, was initially believed to have walked upright in a human manner. Recent studies of Lucy's entire anatomy, not just her knee joints, now show that this is highly improbable. (u) She probably swung from the trees. (v,w) For about 100 years the world was led to believe that Neanderthal man was stooped and ape-like. Recent studies show that this erroneous belief was based upon some Neanderthal men who were crippled with arthritis and rickets. (x-z) Neanderthal man, Heidelberg man, and Cro-Magnon man were completely human. Artists' depictions, especially of the fleshy portions of their bodies, are quite imaginative and are not supported by the evidence. (a1) Furthermore, the dating techniques are questionable. (b1)

20. Many fossils, such as fossilized jelly fish (a,b), show, by the details of their soft, fleshy portions (c), that they were buried rapidly, before they could decay. Many other animals which were buried in mass graves and in twisted and contorted positions suggest violent and rapid burials. These observations, together with the occurrence of compressed fossils and polystrate fossils (d) in Carboniferous, Mesozoic, and Cenozoic formations, are strong evidence that this sedimentary material was deposited rapidly—not over hundreds of millions of years. (Polystrate fossils are those fossils that traverse two or more layers of sedimentary rock.)

21. Bones of many modern-looking humans have been found deep in rock formations that were formed long before man supposedly began to evolve. Examples include: the Calaveras Skull (a-e), the Castenedola Skull (f,g), Reck's Skeleton (h), and many others. (i-m) Other remains present similar problems, such as: the Swanscombe Skull, the Steinheim fossil, and the Vertesszollos fossil. (n,o) These remains are almost always ignored by evolutionists.

22. If evolution happened, the fossil record should show continuous and gradual changes from the bottom to the top layers and between all forms of life. Actually, many gaps and discontinuities appear throughout the fossil record. (a-n) No fossil links have been found between single cell forms of life and invertebrates, invertebrates and vertebrates, fish and amphibians (o), amphibians and reptiles, reptiles and mammals, reptiles and birds (p,q), or primates and other mammals. The fossil record has been studied to such an extent that it is safe to conclude that these gaps are real; they will never be filled. (r)

There is also a sudden explosion of complex species at the bottom of the fossil record. (s) Complex species, such as fish (t), worms, snails, corals, trilobites, jelly fish (u), sponges, mollusks, and brachiopods appear suddenly in the lowest (Cambrian) layers that contain multicellular life. These layers contain representatives of all animal and plant phyla including flowering plants (v,w) and animals with back bones. (x) Insects, a class comprising four-fifths of all known animals (living and extinct), have no evolutionary ancestors. (y) The fossil record does not support evolution.

23. The vertical sequencing of fossils is frequently not in the assumed evolutionary order. (a-d) For example, in the Soviet Union, 86 hoof prints of horses were found in rocks dating back to the dinosaurs. (e) Dinosaur and human-like footprints have also been found together in the Soviet Union. (f) Frequently, ocean-dwelling animals and land animals are fossilized, side-by-side, in the same rock. (g)

24. The vast majority of the sediments, which encase practically all fossils, were laid down through water. The worldwide fossil record is evidence of the rapid death and burial of animal and plant life by a catastrophic flood; it is not evidence of slow change.

NEW RESEARCH SHOWS THAT THE REQUIREMENTS FOR LIFE ARE SO COMPLEX THAT CHANCE AND EVEN BILLIONS OF YEARS CANNOT EXPLAIN IT

25. If the earth, early in its alleged evolution, *had oxygen* in its atmosphere, the chemicals needed for life would have been removed by oxidation. But if there had been *no oxygen*, then there would have been no ozone in the upper atmosphere. Without this ozone, life would be quickly destroyed by the sun's ultraviolet radiation. (a,b) The only way for both ozone and life to be here is for both to have come into existence simultaneously—in other words, CREATION!

26. There have been many imaginative but unsuccessful attempts to explain how just one single protein could form from any of the assumed atmospheres of the early earth. The chemistry of the earth's rocks indicates that oxygen-free atmospheres never existed. (a-c) Furthermore, the necessary chemical reactions all tend to move in the opposite direction from that required by evolution. (d) Even the simplest amino acids would be diluted and destroyed in the atmosphere and oceans, and they could not even approach the required concentrations. (e) Each possible energy source, whether the earth's heat, electrical discharges, or the sun's radiation, would have destroyed the protein products thousands of times faster than they could have been formed. (f-h)

27. If, despite the virtually impossible odds, proteins arose by chance processes, there is not the remotest reason to believe that they could ever form a membrane-encased, self-reproducing, metabolizing living cell. There is no evidence that there are any stable states between

the assumed naturalistic formation of proteins and the formation of the first living cells. No scientist has ever advanced a testable procedure whereby this fantastic jump in complexity could have occurred—even if the universe had been completely filled with proteins. (a)

28. If life is ultimately the result of random chance, then so is thought. Your thoughts—such as what you are now thinking—would, in the final analysis, be a consequence of accidents and therefore would have no validity. (a-c)

29. Techniques now exist for measuring the degree of similarity among most forms of life. These "genetic distances" are calculated by taking a specific protein and examining the slight differences in the sequence of its molecules from one form of life to another. The results of these studies seriously contradict the theory of evolution. (a) There is not a trace of evidence at this molecular level of the traditional evolutionary series: simple sea life—fish—amphibians—reptiles—mammals. (b) In general, each of the many categories of organisms appear to be equally isolated. (c) One computer based study, using the protein "cytochrome c," compared 47 different forms of life. If evolution had actually occurred, this study should have found that the rattlesnake was most closely related to other reptiles. Instead, based on this one protein, the rattlesnake was most similar to the human. (d,e) Hundreds of similar contradictions have also been discovered.

30. The genetic information contained in *each cell* of the human body is roughly equivalent to a library of 4000 (a) volumes. The probability that mutations and natural selection produced this amount of information, assuming that matter and life somehow arose, is essentially zero. (b) It would be analogous to continuing the following procedure until 4000 volumes have been produced: (c,d)

(a) Start with a meaningful phrase.

(b) Retype the phrase but make some errors and insert some additional letters.

(c) Examine the new phrase to see if it is meaningful.

(d) If it is, replace the original phrase with it.

(e) Return to step (b).

To accumulate 4000 volumes that are meaningful, this procedure would have to produce the equivalent of far more than 10^{40000} animal offspring. (Just to begin to understand how large 10^{40000} is, realize that the visible universe has less than 10^{80} *atoms* in it.)

31. DNA can only be produced with the help of certain enzymes. But these enzymes can only be produced at the direction of DNA. (a) Since each requires the other, a satisfactory explanation for the origin of one must also explain the origin of the other. (b,c) Likewise, some

proteins are required to produce other proteins. Apparently, the entire manufacturing system came into existence simultaneously. This implies Creation.

32. Amino acids, when found in nonliving matter, come in two forms that are chemically equivalent: about half can be described as "right-handed" and the other half as "left-handed" (a structural description—one is the mirror image of the other). However, the amino acids that comprise the proteins found in all forms of life, including plants, animals, bacteria, molds, and even viruses, are essentially all left-handed. No natural process known can isolate either the left or the right-handed variety. The mathematical probability that chance processes could produce *just one* tiny protein molecule with only left-handed amino acid is virtually zero. (a,b)

33. The simplest form of life consists of about 600 different protein molecules. The mathematical probability that *just one* molecule could form by the chance arrangement of the proper amino acids is far less than 1 in 10^{450}. (a,b) (The magnitude of the number 10^{450} can begin to be appreciated by realizing that the visible universe is about 10^{28} inches in diameter.)

34. There are many instances where quite different forms of life are completely dependent upon each other. Examples include: fig trees and the fig gall wasp (a,b), the yucca plant and the pronuba moth (c), many parasites and their hosts, and pollen-bearing plants and the honeybee. Even the members of the honeybee family, consisting of the queen, workers, and drones, are interdependent. If one member of each interdependent group evolved first (such as the plant before the animal or even one or two members of the honeybee family before another), it could not have survived. Since all members of the group obviously have survived, they must have come into existence at essentially the same time.

35. If sexual reproduction in plants, animals, and humans is a result of evolutionary sequences, then an absolutely unbelievable series of chance events would have had to occur at each stage. First, the amazingly complex and completely different reproductive systems of the male must have *completely* and *independently* evolved at each stage at about the *same time and place* as those of the female. Just a slight incompleteness in only one of the two would make both reproductive systems useless, and natural selection would oppose their survival. Second, the physical, chemical, and emotional systems of the male and female would also need to be compatible. Third, the complex products of the male reproductive system (pollen or sperm) would need to have an affinity for and a mechanical and chemical compatibility

with the eggs of the female reproductive system. Fourth, the intricate and numerous processes occurring at the molecular level inside the fertilized egg would have to work with fantastic precision—processes that scientists can only describe in an aggregate sense. Finally, the environment of this fertilized egg, from conception until it also reproduced with another sexually capable "brother or sister" that was also "accidentally" produced, would have to be controlled to an unbelievable degree. Either this series of incredible events occurred by random, evolutionary processes or else an Intelligent Designer created sexual reproduction. (a-d)

36. Detailed studies of various animals have revealed certain physical equipment and capabilities that cannot be duplicated by the world's best designers using the most sophisticated technologies. For example, the miniature and reliable sonar systems of the dolphins, porpoises, and whales; the frequency-modulated radar and discrimination system of the bat (a); the efficiency and aerodynamic capabilities of the hummingbird; the control systems, internal ballistics, and redundant navigational systems of many birds and fish; and the self-repair capabilities of practically all forms of life. The many components of each complex system could not have evolved in stages without placing a selective disadvantage on the animal. All evidence points to a Designer.

LIFE SCIENCE CONCLUSION: Following the publishing of *The Origin of Species* by Charles Darwin in 1859, many came to believe that all forms of life had a common ancestor. Those who believed that over long periods of time molecules had turned into man thought there were only a few gaps in this "evolutionary tree"—gaps which would be filled as scientific knowledge increased. Just the opposite has happened. As science has progressed, the "missing links" in this hypothetical tree have multiplied and broadened enormously.

In Darwin's day, all life fell neatly into two categories (or kingdoms): animals and plants. Today we know that life falls into *five* radically different kingdoms, only two of which are animals and plants. This, of course, does not include viruses, which are complex and unique in their own way. In the 1800's, the animal kingdom was divided into four animal phyla; today there are more than forty. New discoveries have caused the gaps in the evolutionary tree to multiply.

Darwin felt that the first living creature came from a "warm little pond." More recent writers have imagined that life arose in some organic soup—a more sophisticated, but equally vague, version of Darwin's warm pond. We now know that the chance formation of the first living cell is a leap of gigantic proportions—vastly more improbably than the evolution of bacteria into humans. In Darwin's day a cell was thought to be about as simple as a ping-pong ball. Today we know that it is a marvelously integrated and complex manufacturing plant with many mysteries yet to be understood. Furthermore, cells come in two radically different types—those with a nucleus and those without. Just the evolutionary leap from one to the other is staggering to imagine. Undoubtedly other gaps or evolutionary hurdles will be found as our understanding of the cell increases.

A century ago there were no sophisticated microscopes. Consequently, the leaps from single to multiple-cell organisms were also underestimated. The development of the computer has likewise given us a partial appreciation of the vast electronics and storage capabilities of the brain. The human eye, which Darwin admitted made him shudder, was only a single jump. It is now known that there are at least a dozen radically different kinds of eyes, each requiring similar jumps if evolution happened. Likewise, the literal leap that we call flight must have evolved—not once, but on at least four different occasions: for birds, insects, mammals, and reptiles. Up until recently, it was thought that sunlight provided the energy for all of life. We now know that at widely separated locations on the dark ocean floor are complex organisms that derive their energy from chemical and thermal energy. For one energy conversion system to evolve into another would be analogous to slowly changing the heating system of a house from gas to electricity by a series of accidents. Furthermore, these accidents must occur by altering one minor component each year without the occupants freezing in the winter. In addition, the entire process must happen several times, each at different locations on the earth. Thousands of other giant leaps must have also occurred if evolution happened: cold-blooded to warm-blooded animals, floating marine plants to vascular plants, placental mammals to marsupials, egg-laying to viviparous animals, and on and on.

The gaps in the fossil record are well-known. A century ago evolutionists argued that these gaps would be filled as knowledge increased. Most paleontologists will now admit that this prediction failed. Of course, the most famous "missing link" is that between man and apes. However, the term is deceiving since there should be not one, but thousands of intermediate links if the evolutionary tree connects man and apes in spite of their many linguistic, social, mental, and physical differences.

Scientific advancements have shown us that evolution is even more ridiculous than it appeared to people in Darwin's day. It is a theory without a mechanism. Not even appeals to long periods of time will allow simple organisms to jump gaps and become more complex. In fact, as you will see, long periods of time make it even less likely that evolutionary leaps would occur. All the experiments which many hoped would show macroevolution have failed. The arguments used by Darwin and his followers are now discredited or, at best, in dispute even among evolutionists. Finally, the research of the last several decades has shown that the requirements for life are incredibly complex. The theory of organic evolution certainly appears to be invalid.

We will now see several other serious difficulties as we leave the life sciences and examine the astronomical sciences. If the earth, the solar system, our galaxy, or even the heavier chemical elements could not evolve, then organic evolution could not even begin. This appears to be the case.

NATURALISTIC EXPLANATIONS FOR THE EVOLUTION OF THE SOLAR SYSTEM AND UNIVERSE ARE UNSCIENTIFIC AND HOPELESSLY INADEQUATE.

Many undisputed observations of our solar system contradict the current theories on how the solar system evolved. (a-c) According to these evolutionary theories:

37. All planets should rotate on their axes in the same direction, but Venus, Uranus, and Pluto rotate backwards. (d)

38. All 44 moons in our solar system should revolve in the same direction, but at least six revolve backwards. (d) Furthermore, Jupiter, Saturn, and Neptune have moons going in both directions.

39. The orbits of these 44 moons should all lie in the equatorial plane of the planet they orbit (d), but many, including the earth's moon, are in highly inclined orbits. (d)

40. The material of the earth (as well as Mars, Venus, and Mercury) should almost all be hydrogen and helium—similar to that of the sun and the rest of the visible universe; actually, much less than 1% of the earth's mass is hydrogen or helium. (d,e)

41. The sun should have 700 times more angular momentum than the planets; in fact, the planets have 200 more times more angular momentum than the sun. (d,e)

42. The sun's tidal forces are so strong that dust clouds or gas clouds lying within the orbit of Jupiter could never condense to form planets. (a)

43. Saturn's rings could not have formed from the disintegration of a former satellite or from the capture of external material; the particles

in these rings are too small and too evenly distributed throughout orbits that are too circular. Therefore, the rings appear to be remnants of Saturn's creation.

44. Naturalistic theories on the moon's origin are highly speculative and completely inadequate. (a,b) The moon was not torn from the earth, nor did it congeal from the same material as the earth since its orbital plane is too highly inclined. Furthermore, the relative abundances of its elements are too dissimilar from those of the earth. (c) The moon's circular orbit is also strong evidence that it was never torn from nor captured by the earth. (d-f) If the moon formed from particles orbiting the earth, other particles should be easily visible inside the moon's orbit; none are. If the moon was not pulled from the earth, was not built up from smaller particles near its present orbit, and was not captured from outside its present orbit, only one hypothesis remains: the moon was created in its present orbit.

45. No scientific theory exists to explain the origin of matter, space, or time. Since each is intimately related to or even defined in terms of the other, a satisfactory explanation for the origin of one must also explain the origin of the others. (a) Naturalistic explanations have completely failed.

46. The First Law of Thermodynamics states that the total amount of energy in the universe, or in any isolated part of it, remains constant. This law states that although energy (or its mass equivalent) can change form, it is not now being created or destroyed. Countless experiments have verified this. A corollary of the First Law is that natural processes cannot create energy. Consequently, energy must have been created in the past by some agency or power outside of and independent of the natural universe. Furthermore, if natural processes could not produce the relatively simple inorganic portion of the universe, then it is even more likely that natural processes could not explain the organic (or living) portion of the universe.

47. If the entire universe is an isolated system, then, according to the Second Law of Thermodynamics, the energy in the universe that is available for useful work has always been decreasing. However, as one goes back further in time, the amount of energy available for useful work would eventually exceed the total energy in the universe that, according to the First Law of Thermodynamics, remains constant. This is an impossible condition. Therefore, it implies that the universe had a beginning.

48. Heat always flows from hot bodies to cold bodies. If the universe were infinitely old, the temperature throughout the universe should be uniform. Since the temperature of the universe is not

uniform, the universe is not infinitely old. Therefore, the universe had a beginning. (a)

49. A further consequence of the Second Law is that when the universe began, it was in a more organized state than it is today—not in a highly disorganized state as assumed by evolutionists and proponents of the Big Bang Theory.

50. The cosmic background radiation is considered by many to be the major evidence supporting the Big Bang Theory. However, recent measurements of this radiation above the earth's atmosphere indicate that this background radiation is not consistent with the Big Bang hypothesis. (a-c) Furthermore, the abundance of helium in the universe is not consistent with the Big Bang. (d,e) Furthermore, if the Big Bang occurred, the universe should not contain lumpy (f-h) or rotating bodies. Since both types of bodies are seen (i), it is doubtful that the Big Bang occurred.

51. Detailed analyses indicate that stars could not have formed from interstellar gas clouds. To do so, either by first forming dust particles (a,b) or by direct gravitational collapse of the gas, would require vastly more time than the alleged age of the universe. An obvious alternative is that stars were created.

52. If stars evolve, we should see about as many star births as star deaths. The deaths of stars are bright and sudden events called "supernovas." Similarly, the birth of a star should be accompanied by the appearance of new star light on the many photographic plates made decades earlier. Instruments should also be able to detect dust falling into the new star. We have *never* seen a star born, but we have seen thousands of stars die. There is no evidence that stars evolve. (a)

53. Stellar evolution is assumed in estimating the age of stars. These age estimates are then used to establish a framework for stellar evolution. This is circular reasoning. (a)

54. There is no evidence that galaxies evolve from one type to another. (a,b) Furthermore, if galaxies are billions of years old, orbital mechanics requires that neither the arms in spiral galaxies nor the bar in barred spiral galaxies should have maintained their shape. (c) Since they have maintained their shape, either galaxies are young, or unknown physical phenomena are occurring within galaxies. (d,e)

TECHNIQUES THAT ARGUE FOR AN OLD EARTH ARE EITHER ILLOGICAL OR ARE BASED ON UNREASONABLE ASSUMPTIONS.

55. Any estimated date prior to the beginning of written records must necessarily assume that the dating clock has operated at a known

rate, that the initial setting of the clock is known, and that the clock has not been disturbed. These assumptions are almost always unstated or overlooked.

56. A major assumption that underlies all radioactive dating techniques is that the rates of decay, which have been essentially constant over the past 90 years, have also been constant over the past 4,600,000,000 years. This bold, critical, and untestable assumption is made even though no one knows what causes radioactive decay. Furthermore, there is evidence suggesting that radioactive decay has not always been constant but has varied by many orders of magnitude from that observed today. (a,b)

57. The public has been greatly misled concerning the consistency, reliability, and trustworthiness of radiometric dating techniques (the Potassium-Argon method, the Rubidium-Strontium method, and the Uranium-Thorium-Lead method). Many of the published dates can be checked by comparisons with the assumed ages for the fossils that sometimes lie above and below radiometrically dated rock. In over 400 of these published checks (about half), the radiometrically determined ages were at least one geologic age in error—indicating major errors in methodology. An unanswered question is, "How many other dating checks were *not published* because they too were in error?" (a,b)

58. Radiocarbon dating, which has been accurately calibrated by counting the rings of living trees that are up to 3,500 years old, is unable to extend this accuracy to date more ancient organic remains. A few people have claimed that ancient wood exists which will permit this calibration to be extended even further back in time, but they have not published their raw data. On the other hand, measurements made at hundreds of sites worldwide (a,b) indicate that the concentration of radiocarbon in the atmosphere rose quite rapidly at some time prior to 3,500 years ago. If this happened, the maximum possible radiocarbon age obtainable with the standard techniques (approximately 50,000 years) could easily correspond to a *true* age of 5,000 years.

59. Radiohalos are tiny spheres of discoloration produced by the radioactive decay of particles that are encased in various crystals. Radiohalos are strong evidence that the earth's crust was never in a molten state. Based upon the specific patterns seen in many of these rocks, it appears that these rocks came into existence almost instantaneously—in other words, CREATION! (a,b)

60. Geological formations are almost always dated by their fossil content, especially by certain *index fossils* of extinct plants and animals. The age of the fossil is derived from the assumed evolutionary sequence, but the evolutionary sequence is based on the fossil record.

This reasoning is circular. (a-e) Furthermore, this procedure has produced many contradictory results. (f)

61. Practically nowhere on the earth can one find the so-called "geologic column." (a) In fact, on the continents, over half the "geologic periods" are usually missing, and 15-20% of the earth has less than one-third of these periods. (b) Even within the Grand Canyon, over 100 million years of this imaginary column are missing. Using the assumed geologic column to date fossils and rocks is fallacious.

62. Estimated old ages for the earth are frequently based on "clocks" that today are ticking at very slow rates. For example, coral growth rates were for many years thought to be very slow, implying that some coral reefs must be hundreds of thousands of years old. More accurate measurements of these rates under favorable growth conditions now show us that no known coral formation need be over 3,500 years old. (a) A similar comment can be made for the growth rates of stalactites and stalagmites. (b)

63. Many different people have found, at different times and places, man-made artifacts encased in coal. Examples include an 8-carat gold chain (a-c), a spoon (b), a thimble, an iron pot (d), a bell, and other objects of obvious human manufacture. Many other "out of place artifacts" such as a metallic vase, a screw, nails (a), a strange coin (c), a doll (c,e), and others (f) have been found buried deeply in solid rock. By evolutionary dating techniques, these objects would be hundreds of millions of years old, but man supposedly did not begin to evolve until 2-4 million years ago. Again, something is wrong.

64. In rock formations in Utah (a), Kentucky (b), Missouri (c), and possibly Pennsylvania (d), human-like *footprints* that are supposedly 150-600 million years old have been found and examined by different authorities. There appears to be a drastic error in chronology.

65. Since there is no worldwide unconformity in the earth's sedimentary strata, the entire geologic record must have been deposited rapidly. (An *unconformity* is an erosional surface between two adjacent rock formations representing a time break of unknown duration.) *Conformities* imply a continuous and rapid deposition. Since one can trace continuous paths from the bottom to the top of the geologic record that avoid these unconformities, the sediments along those paths must have been deposited continuously. (a)

**MOST DATING TECHNIQUES INDICATE THAT
THE EARTH, THE SOLAR SYSTEM, AND
THE UNIVERSE ARE YOUNG**

For the last 130 years the age of the earth, as assumed by evolutionists, has been doubling at a rate of once every 20 years. In fact since 1900, this age has multiplied by a factor of 100!

Evolution requires an old earth, an old solar system, and an old universe. Without billions of years, virtually all informed evolutionists will admit that their theory is dead. But by hiding the "origins question" behind the veil of vast periods of time, the unsolvable problems of evolution become difficult for scientists to see and laymen to imagine. Our media and textbooks have implied for over a century that this almost unimaginable age is correct, but rarely do they examine the shaky assumptions and growing body of contrary evidence. Therefore, most people instinctively believe that the earth and universe are old, and it is disturbing (at least initially) to hear evidence that they are probably quite young.

Actually most dating techniques indicate that the earth and solar system are young—possibly less than 10,000 years old. Listed below are just a few of these evidences.

66. The radioactive decay of just uranium and thorium would produce all of the atmospheric helium in only 40,000 years. Detailed experimentation has shown that there is no known means by which large amounts of helium can escape from the atmosphere, even when considering the low atomic weight of helium. The atmosphere appears to be young. (a,b)

67. Lead diffuses (or leaks) from zircon crystals at known rates that increase with temperature. Since these crystals are found at different depths in the earth, those at greater depths and temperatures should have less lead. Even if the earth's crust is just a fraction of the age that is claimed by evolutionists, there should be a measurable difference in the lead content of zircons throughout the top 4000 meters. Actually, no measurable difference is found. (a,b) Similar conclusions are reached from a study of the helium contained in these same zircon crystals. (c) In fact, these helium studies lead to a conclusion that the earth's crust is only thousands of years old. (d)

68. The occurrence of abnormally high gas and oil pressures within relatively permeable rock implies that these fluids were formed or encased less than 10,000 years ago. If these hydrocarbons had been trapped *over* 10,000 years ago, leakage would have dropped the pressure to a level far below what it is today. (a)

69. Over twenty-seven billion tons of river sediments are entering the oceans each year. Probably, the rate of sediment transport was even greater in the past as the looser top soil was removed and as erosion smoothed out the earth's relief. Even if erosion has been constant, the sediments that are now on the ocean floor would have accumulated in

only 30 million years. Therefore, the oceans cannot be hundreds of millions of years old. (a)

70. The continents are being eroded at a rate that would level them in much less than twenty-five million years. (a,b) However, evolutionists believe that the fossils of land animals and plants that are at high elevations have been there for over 300 million years. Something is wrong.

71. The rate at which elements such as copper, gold, tin, lead, silicon, mercury, uranium, and nickel are entering the oceans is very rapid when compared with the small quantities of these elements already in the oceans. There is no known means by which large amounts of these elements can precipitate out of the oceans. Therefore, the oceans must be very much younger than a million years.

72. Meteorites are falling at a fairly steady rate onto the earth. This rate of influx was probably much greater in the past since much of the original meteoritic material has been purged from the solar system. Experts have therefore expressed surprise that meteorites are only found in relatively young sediments very near the earth's surface. (a-d) Even the meteoritic particles in ocean sediments tend to be concentrated in the top-most layers. (e) If the earth's sediments, which average about a mile in thickness on the continents, were deposited over hundreds of millions of years, as evolutionists believe, many iron meteorites should be well below the earth's surface. Since this is not the case, the sediments appear to have been deposited rapidly. Furthermore, since no meteorites are found immediately above the basement rocks on which these sediments rest, these basement rocks could not have been exposed to meteoritic bombardment for any great length of time.

73. The rate at which meteoritic dust is accumulating on the earth is such that after five billion years, the equivalent of over 16 feet of this dust should have accumulated. Because this dust is high in nickel, there should be an abundance of nickel in the crustal rocks of the earth. No such concentration has been found—on land or in the oceans. Consequently, the earth appears to be young. (a-c)

74. Direct measurements of the earth's magnetic field over the past 140 years show a steady and rapid decline in its strength. This decay pattern is consistent with the theoretical view that there is an electrical current inside the earth which produces the magnetic field. If this view is correct, then just 20,000 years ago the electrical current would have been so vast that the earth's structure could not have survived the heat produced. This implies that the earth could not be older than 20,000 years. (a)

75. If the earth were initially molten, it would have cooled to its present condition in much less than 4.6 billion years. This conclusion holds even after one makes liberal assumptions on the amount of heat generated by radioactive decay within the earth. (a,b) The known temperature pattern inside the earth is only consistent with a young earth.

76. Since 1754, observations of the moon's orbit indicate that it is receding from earth. (a,b) As tidal friction gradually slows the earth's spin, the laws of physics require the moon to recede from the earth. However, the moon should have moved from near the earth's surface to its present distance in several billion years less time than the 4.6 billion year age that evolutionists assume for the earth and moon. Consequently, the earth-moon system must be much younger than evolutionists assume.

77. If the moon were billions of years old, it should have accumulated a thick layer of dust from outer space. Before instruments were placed on the moon, NASA and outside scientists (a) were very concerned that our astronauts would sink into a sea of dust—possibly a mile in thickness. This did not happen. There is very little space dust on the moon. In fact, after examining the rocks and dust brought back from the moon, it was learned that only about 1/60th of the one or two inch surface layer came from outer space. (b,c) Recent measurements (d) of the influx rate also do not support the thin layer of meteoritic dust on the moon, even if this rate were no higher in the past. Of course the rate of dust accumulation on the moon should have been much greater in the past. Conclusion: the moon is probably quite young.

78. The moon has a magnetic field and is still warm. (a) This suggests that the moon is young.

79. As short period comets pass near the sun, some of their mass vaporizes and forms a long tail. Nothing should remain of these comets after about 10,000 years. There is certainly no shell of cometary material surrounding the solar system, (a) and there are no known ways to add comets to the solar system. In fact, the gravitational attractions of the larger planets tend to expel comets from the solar system. (a) Consequently, comets and the solar system appear to be less than 10,000 year old. (b-e)

80. Jupiter and Saturn each radiate more than twice the energy they receive from the sun. (a-b) Venus also radiates too much energy. (c) Calculations show that it is very unlikely that this energy comes from nuclear fusion, (d) radioactive decay, gravitational contraction, or phase changes within those planets. The only other conceivable explanation is that these planets have not existed long enough to cool off. (e,f)

81. The sun's gravitational field acts as a giant vacuum cleaner that sweeps up about 100,000 tons of micrometeoroids per day. If the solar system were older than 10,000 years, no micrometeroids should remain near the center of the solar system since there is no significant source of replenishment. A large disk-shaped cloud of these particles is orbiting the sun. Conclusion: the solar system is less than 10,000 years old. (a,b)

82. The sun's radiation applies an outward force on very small particles orbiting the sun. Particles less than 100,000th of a centimeter in diameter should have been "blown out" of the solar system if the solar system were billions of years old. These particles are still orbiting the sun. (a) Conclusion: the solar system is young.

83. If the sun, when it first began to radiate, had any nonnuclear sources of energy, they would have been depleted in much less than ten million years. Theory (a) and experiment (b) indicate that nuclear reactions are not the predominant energy source for the sun. Our star, the sun, must therefore be young (less than ten million years old). If the sun is young, then so is the earth.

84. Since 1836, over one hundred different observers at the Royal Greenwich Observatory and the U.S. Naval Observatory have made *direct* visual measurements that indicate that the sun's diameter is shrinking at a rate of about .1% each century or about five feet per hour! Furthermore, records of solar eclipses indicate that this rapid shrinking has been going on for at least the past 400 years. (a) Several *indirect* techniques also confirm this gravitational collapse, although these inferred collapse rates are only about 1/7th as much. (b,c) Using the most conservative data, one must conclude that had the sun existed a million years ago, it would have been so large that it would have heated the earth so much that life could not have survived. Yet, evolutionists say that a million years ago all the present forms of life were essentially as they are now, having completed their evolution that began a *thousand* million years ago.

85. Stars that are moving in the same direction at significantly different speeds frequently travel in closely-spaced clusters. (a) This would not be the case if they had been traveling for billions of years because even the slightest difference in their velocities would disperse them after such great periods of time. Similar observations have been made of galaxy and of galaxy-quasar combinations that apparently have vastly different velocities but which appear to be connected. (b-d)

86. Computer simulations of the motions of spiral galaxies show them to be highly unstable; they should completely change their shape in only a small fraction of the assumed age of the universe. (a) The simplest explanation for the existence of so many spiral galaxies,

including our own Milky Way Galaxy, is that they and the universe are much younger than has been assumed.

88. Galaxies are often found in tight clusters that contain hundreds of galaxies. The velocities of individual galaxies within these clusters are so high in comparison to the calculated mass of the entire cluster that these clusters should be flying apart. However, since the galaxies within clusters are so close together, they could not have been flying apart for very long. A 10-20 billion year old universe is completely inconsistent with what we see. (a-d)

All dating techniques, especially the *few* that suggest vast ages, presume that a process observed today has always proceeded at a known rate. In many cases this assumption may be grossly inaccurate. For the many dating "clocks" that show a young earth and a young universe, a much better understanding usually exists for the various mechanisms that drive these clocks. Furthermore, the extrapolation process is over a much shorter time and is therefore more likely to be correct.

For the person who has always been told that the earth is billions of years old, this contrary evidence is understandably disturbing. But can you imagine how disturbing this evidence is to the evolutionist?

ARCHAEOLOGICAL EVIDENCE INDICATES THAT NOAH'S ARK PROBABLY EXISTS (a-g)

88. Ancient historians such as Josephus, the Jewish-Roman historian, and Berosus of the Chaldeans mentioned in their writings that the Ark existed. Marco Polo also stated that the Ark was reported to be on a mountain in greater Armenia.

89. In about 1856, a team of three skeptical British scientists and two Armenian guides climbed to Ararat to demonstrate that the Ark did not exist. The Ark was supposedly found, but the British scientists threatened to kill the guides if they reported it. Years later one of the Armenians (then living in the United States) and one of the British scientists independently reported that they had actually located the Ark.

90. Sir James Bryce, a noted British scholar and traveler of the mid-nineteenth century, conducted extensive library research concerning the Ark. He became convinced that the Ark was preserved on Mount Ararat. Finally, in 1876, he ascended to the summit of the mountain and found, at the 13,000 foot level (2,000 feet above the timber line), a large piece of hand-tooled wood that he believed was from the Ark.

91. In 1883, a series of newspaper articles reported that a team of Turkish commissioners, while investigating avalanche conditions on

Mount Ararat, unexpectedly came upon the Ark projecting out of the melting ice at the end of an unusually warm summer. They claimed that they entered and examined a portion of the Ark.

92. In the unusually warm summer of 1902, an Armenian boy, Georgie Hagopian, and his uncle climbed to the Ark that was reportedly sticking out of an ice pack. The boy climbed over the Ark and examined it in great detail. In 1904 Hagopian visited the Ark for a second time. Shortly before his death in 1972, a tape recording was made of his detailed testimony. This recording has undergone voice analyzer tests which indicate that his account is quite credible. (h)

93. A Russian pilot, flying over Ararat in World War I (1915), thought he saw the Ark. The news of his discovery reached the Czar, who dispatched a large expedition to the site. The soldiers located and explored the boat, but before they could report back to the Czar, the Russian Revolution of 1917 had begun. Their report disappeared, and the soldiers were scattered. Some of them eventually reached the United States. Various relatives and friends have confirmed this report.

94. At about the time of the Russian sighting, five Turkish soldiers, crossing Mount Ararat, claim to have seen the Ark; however, they did not report their story until 30 years later when they offered to guide an American expedition to the site. The expedition did not materialize, and their services were not sought until after their deaths.

95. During World War II, a group of Russian flyers, on at least two occasions, took aerial photographs that showed the Ark protruding out of the ice. In Berlin, after the war, these photos were shown to an American doctor who subsequently disclosed this story.

96. An oil geologist, George Greene, in 1953 took a number of photographs of the Ark from a helicopter. After returning to the United States, Greene showed his photographs to many people but was unable to raise financial backing for a ground-based expedition. Finally, he went to South America where he was killed. Although the pictures have not been located, over thirty people have given sworn written testimony that they saw these photographs that clearly showed the Ark protruding from the melting ice field at the edge of a precipice.

There are many other stories in which people claim to have seen the Ark. Some of these are of questionable validity, and others are inconsistent with many of the known details. Only the most credible are summarized above.

MANY OF THE EARTH'S PREVIOUSLY UNEXPLAINABLE FEATURES CAN BE EXPLAINED ONLY BY THIS FLOOD (a)

The origin of each of the following features of the earth is a subject of controversy within the earth sciences. Each typically involves numerous hypotheses and unexplainable aspects. Yet all of these features can be veiwed as direct consequences of a singular and unrepeatable event—a cataclysmic flood whose waters burst forth from worldwide, subterranean, and interconnected chambers with an energy release in excess of one trillion megatons of TNT. The cause and effect sequence of the events involved phenomena that are either well understood or are observable in modern times.

97. Glaciers and the Ice Age
98. Frozen mammoths
99. Salt domes
100. Continental drift
101. Coal formations
102. Mountains
103. Overthrusts
104. Extinction of the dinosaurs
105. Ocean trenches
106. Submarine canyons
107. Mid-oceanic ridge
108. Magnetic patterns of the ocean floor
109. Strata
110. Continental shelves and slopes
111. Submarine volcanoes and guyots
112. Metamorphic rock

THE SEEMINGLY IMPOSSIBLE EVENTS OF A WORLDWIDE FLOOD ARE REALLY QUITE PLAUSIBLE IF EXAMINED CLOSELY

113. Every major mountain range on the earth contains fossils of sea life.

114. Practically every culture on earth has legends telling of a traumatic flood in which only a few humans survived in a large boat. (a)

115. The majority of the earth's mountains were formed after most of the sediments were deposited. If these mountains were again flattened out (while the ocean basins were allowed to rise in compensation for this downward flow of mass), the oceans would flood the entire earth. Therefore, there is enough water on the earth to cover the smaller mountains that existed prior to the flood.

116. Seeds can still germinate after soaking for a year in salt water. (a)

Reference List

2. a) Monroe W. Strickberger, *Genetica*, 2nd edition (New York: Macmillan Publishing Co., 1976), p. 812.
   b) Alfred Russell Wallace, who along with Charles Darwin coauthored the theory of evolution, was opposed to Mendel's laws of genetics. Wallace recognized that Mendel's experiments showed that the general characteristics of an organism remained within distinct boundaries. In a letter to Dr. Archdall Reid on December 28, 1909, Wallace wrote:
   > "But on the general relation of Mendelism to Evolution I have come to a very definite conclusion. This is, that it has no relation whatever to the evolution of species or higher groups, but is really antagonistic to such evolution!"
   >
   > Alfred Russell Wallace
   > *Letters and Reminiscences* by James Marchant
   > (New York: Harper and Brothers, 1916), p. 340.
   c) Francis Hitching, *The Neck of the Giraffe: Where Darwin Went Wrong* (New Haven, Connecticut: Ticknor and Fields, 1982), p. 55.
   d) "All competent biologists acknowledge the limited nature of the variation breeders can produce, although they do not like to discuss it much when grinding the evolutionary ax."
   > William R. Fix
   > *The Bone Peddlers: Selling Evolution*
   > (New York: Macmillan, 1984), pp. 184-85.
   e) "A rule that all breeders recognize, is that there are fixed limits to the amount of change that can be produced."
   > Lane P. Lester and Raymond Bohlin
   > *The Natural Limits to Biological Change*
   > (Grand Rapids: Zondervan, 1984), p. 96.
   f) Norman Macbeth, *Darwin Retired: An Appeal to Reason* (Ipswich, Massachusetts: Gambit, 1971), p. 36.
3. a) N. Heribert Nilsson, *Synthetische Artbildung* (Lund Sweden: Verlag CWK Gleerup, 1953), pp. 1144-47.
5. a) "Ultimately, all variation is, of course, due to mutation."
   > Ernst Mayr, as contained in Paul S. Moorhead and Martin M. Kaplan, editors, *Mathematical Challenges to the Neo-Darwinian Interpretation of Evolution*, Proceedings of a symposium held at the Wistar Institute of Anatomy and Biology, April 25 and 26, 1966 (Philadelphia: The Wistar Institute Press, 1967), p. 50.
   b) "Although mutation is the ultimate source of all genetic variation, it is a relatively rare event, ..."
   > Francisco J. Ayala
   > "The Mechanism of Evolution," *Scientific American*, September 1978, p. 63.

c) "Mutations are more than just sudden changes in heredity; they also affect viability, and, to the best of our knowledge, invariably affect it adversely."
> C. P. Martin (McGill University)
> "A Non-Geneticist Looks at Evolution," *American Scientist*, January 1953, p. 102.

"Mutation does produce hereditary changes, but the mass of evidence shows that all, or almost all, known mutations are unmistakably pathological and the few remaining ones are highly suspect."
> C. P. Martin, p. 103

"[although mutations have produced some desirable breeds of animals and plants,] all mutations seem to be in the nature of injuries that, to some extent, impair the fertility and viability of the affected organisms. I doubt if among the many thousands of known mutant types one can be found which is superior to the wild type in its normal environment, only very few can be named which are superior to the wild type in a strange environment."
> C. P. Martin, p. 100.

d) "The process of mutation is the only source of the raw materials of genetic variability, and hence of evolution . . . The mutants which arise are, with rare exceptions, deleterious to their carriers, at least in the environments which the species normally encounters."
> Theodosius Dobzhansky
> "On Methods of Evolutionary Biology and Anthropology," *American Scientist*, Winter, December 1957, p. 385.

e) "If we say that it is only by chance that they [mutations] are useful, we are still speaking too leniently. In general, they are useless, detrimental, or lethal."
> W. R. Thompson
> "Introduction to *The Origin of Species*," by Charles Darwin; Everyman No. 811 Library (New York: E. P. Dutton & Sons, 1956 reprint of 1928 edition), p. 10.

f) ". . . we could still be quite sure on theoretical grounds that mutants would usually be detrimental. For a mutation is a random change of a highly organized, reasonably smoothly functioning living body. A random change in the highly integrated system of chemical processes which constitute life is almost certain to impair it—just as a random interchange of connections in a television set is not likely to improve the picture."
> James F. Crow
> (Professor of Genetics, University of Wisconsin)
> "Genetic Effects of Radiation," *Bulletin of the Atomic Scientists*, Vol. 14, 1958, pp. 19-20.

g) "The one systematic effect of mutation seems to be a tendency towards degeneration."
Sewall Wright
"The Statistical Consequences of Mendelian Heredity in Relation to Speciation," in *The New Systematics* edited by Julian Huxley (London: Oxford University Press, 1949), p. 174.

h) In discussing the many mutations needed to produce a new organ, Koestler says that
"Each mutation occurring alone would be wiped out before it could be combined with the others. They are all interdependent. The doctrine that their coming together was due to a series of blind coincidences is an affront not only to common sense but to the basic principles of scientific explanation."
Arthur Koestler
The Ghost in the Machine (New York: Macmillan, 1968), p. 129.

6. a) "Do we, therefore, ever see mutations going about the business of producing new structures for selection to work on? No nascent organ has ever been observed emerging, though their origin in prefunctional form is basic to evolutionary theory. Some should be visible today, occurring in organisms at various stages up to integration of a functional new system, but we don't see them: there is no sign at all of this kind of radical novelty. Neither observation nor controlled experiment has shown natural selection manipulating mutations so as to produce a new gene, hormone, enzyme system or organ."
Michael Pitman
Adam and Evolution (London: Rider, 1984), pp. 67-68.

b) "There is no single instance where it can be maintained that any of the mutants studied has a higher vitality than the mother species."
N. Heribert Nilsson
(Lund University, Sweden), *Synthetische Artbildung* (Lund Sweden: Verlag CWK Gleerup, 1953), p. 1157.
"IT IS, THEREFORE, ABSOLUTELY IMPOSSIBLE TO BUILD A CURRENT EVOLUTION ON MUTATIONS OR ON RECOMBINATIONS. (emphasis his)
N. Heribert Nilsson, p. 1186.

c) "No matter how numerous they may be, mutations do not produce any kind of evolution."
Pierre-Paul Grasse
Evolution of Living Organisms (New York: Academic Press, 1977), p. 88.

d) "It is equally true that nobody has produced even a species by the selection of micromutations."
   Richard B. Goldschmidt
   "Evolution, As Viewed by One Geneticist," *American Scientist*, Vol. 40, January 1952, p. 94.
e) "If life really depends on each gene being as unique as it appears to be, then it is too unique to come into being by chance mutations."
   Frank B. Salisbury
   (Plant Science Department, Utah State University)
   "Natural Selection and the Complexity of the Gene," *Nature*, Vol. 224, 25 October 1969, p. 342.

7. a) Strickberger, p. 44.
   b) "Most mutants which arise in any organism are more or less disadvantageous to their possessors. The classical mutants obtained in Drosophila [the fruit fly] usually show deterioration, breakdown, or disappearance of some organs. Mutants are known which diminish the quantity or destroy the pigment in the eyes, and in the body reduce the wings, eyes, bristles, legs. Many mutants are, in fact, lethal to their possessors. Mutants which equal the normal fly in vigor are a minority, and mutants that would make a major improvement of the normal organization in the normal environments are unknown."
      Theodosius Dobzhansky
      Evolution, Genetics, and Man (New York: John Wiley & Sons, 1955). p. 105.
   c) "A review of known facts about their [mutated fruit flies] ability to survive has led to no other conclusion than that they are always constitutionally weaker than their parent form or species, and in a population with free competition they are eliminated. Therefore they are never found in nature (e.g. not a single one of the several hundreds of Drosophila mutations), and therefore they are able to appear only in the favourable environment of the experimental field or laboratory..."
      Heribert Nilsson, p. 1186.
   d) "In the best-known organisms, like Drosophila, innumerable mutants are known. If we were to combine a thousand or more of such mutants in a single individual, this still would have no resemblance whatsoever to any type known as a species in nature."
      Richard B. Goldschmidt. p. 94.
   e) "It is a striking, but not much mentioned fact that, though geneticists have been breeding fruit-flies for sixty years or more in labs all round the world—flies which produce a new generation every eleven days—they have never yet seen the emergence of a new

species or even a new enzyme."
Gordon Rattray Taylor
The Great Evolution Mystery (New York: Harper and Row, 1983), p. 48.
f) "Fruit flies refuse to become anything but fruit flies under any circumstances yet devised."
Francis Hitching, p. 61.
8. a) "Was the eye contrived without skill in optics, and the ear without knowledge of sounds?"
Sir Isaac Newton
Opticks (New York: McGraw-Hill, 1931), pp. 369-70.
b) "Certainly there are those who argue that the universe evolved out of a random process, but what random process could produce the brain of a man or the system of the human eye?"
Wernher von Braun (probably the one rocket scientist most responsible for the United States placing men on the moon), cited by Bill Keith, *Scopes II: The Great Debate* (Huntington House, 1982), p. 25.
c) "It must be admitted, however, that it is a considerable strain on one's credulity to assume that finely balanced systems such as certain sense organs (the eye of vertebrates, or the bird's feather) could be improved by random mutations. This is even more true for some of the ecological chain relationships (the famous yucca moth case, and so forth). However, the objectors to random mutations have so far been unable to advance any alternative explanation that was supported by substantial evidence."
Ernst Mayr
Systematics and the Origin of Species (New York: Dover Publications, 1942), p. 296.
d) Marlyn E. Clark, *Our Amazing Circulatory System*, Technical Monograph No. 5 (San Diego: Creation-Life Publishers, 1976).
9. a) "Thus so far as concerns the major groups of animals, the creationists seem to have the better of the argument. There is not the slightest evidence that any one of the major groups arose from any other. Each is a special animal complex related, more or less closely, to all the rest, and appearing, therefore, as a special and distinct creation."
Austin Clark F.R.G.S.
Quarterly Review of Biology, Vol. 3, No. 4, December 1928, p. 539.
b) "When we descend to details, we can prove that no one species has changed; nor can we prove that the supposed changes are beneficial, which is the groundwork of the theory [of evolution]."
Charles Darwin
The Life and Letters of Charles Darwin, edited by Francis

Darwin (New York: D. Appleton & Company, 1898), Vol. 2, p. 210.
- c) "Indeed, the isolation and distinctness of different types of organisms and the existence of clear discontinuities in nature have been self-evident for centuries, even to non-biologists."
Michael Denton
Evolution: A Theory in Crisis (London: Burnett Books, 1985), p. 105.
- d) "The fact that all the individual species must be stationed at the extreme periphery of such logic trees merely emphasized the fact that the order of nature betrays no hint of natural evolutionary sequential arrangements, revealing species to be related as sisters or cousins but *never* as ancestors and descendants as is required by evolution."
Denton, p. 132.
10. a) William Paley, *Natural Theology*, 1802 (reprinted Houston, Texas: St. Thomas Press, 1972).
This work by Paley, which contains many powerful arguments for a designer or Creator, is a classic among scientific literature. Some people might feel that its date of original publication (1802) makes it completely out of date. Not so. Hoyle and Wickramasinghe compared Darwin's ideas with those of Paley as follows:
"The speculations of *The Origin of Species* turned out to be wrong, as we have seen in this chapter. It is ironic that the scientific facts throw Darwin out, but leave William Paley, a figure of fun to the scientific world for more than a century, still in the tournament with a chance of being the ultimate winner."
Sir Fred Hoyle and N. Chandra Wickramasinghe
Evolution from Space (New York: Simon and Schuster, 1981), pp. 96-97.
- b) "To suppose that the eye with all its inimitable contrivances for adjusting the focus to different distances, for admitting different amounts of light, and for the correction of spherical and chromatic aberration, could have been formed by natural selection, seems, I freely confess, absurd in the highest degree."
Charles Darwin
The Origin of Species (The Macmillan Company, 1927), p. 175.
12. a) David C. C. Watson, *The Great Brain Robbery* (Chicago: Moody Press, 1976), pp. 83-89.
- b) Henry M. Morris, "Language, Creation and the Inner Man," *ICR Impact*, No. 28 (El Cajon, California: Institute for Creation Research).
- c) Les Bruce, Jr., "On the Origin of Language," *ICR Impact*, No. 44 (El Cajon, California: Institute for Creation Research).

13. a) Arthur Custance, *Genesis and Early Man* (Grand Rapids: Zondervan Publishing House, 1975), pp. 250-71.
15. a) "... it is unscientific to maintain that morphology may be used to prove relationships and evolution of the higher categories of units,..."
Heribert Nilsson, p. 1186.
   b) "Therefore, homologous structures need not be controlled by identical genes, and homology of phenotypes does not imply similarity of genotypes."
"It is now clear that the pride with which it was assumed that the inheritance of homologous structures from a common ancestor explained homology was misplaced; for such inheritance cannot be described to identity of genes."
"But if it is true that through the genetic code, genes for enzymes that synthesize proteins which are responsible (in a manner still unknown in embryology) for the differentiation of the various parts in their normal manner, what mechanism can it be that results in the production of homologous organs, the same 'patterns,' in spite of their *not* being controlled by the same genes? I asked this question in 1938, and it has not been answered." [Nor has it been answered today.—W.T.B.]
Sir Gavin R. de Beer
(formerly Professor of Embryology in the University of London and Director of the British Museum of Natural History), *Homology, An Unsolved Problem* (London: Oxford University Press, 1971), pp. 15-16.
   c) Fix, pp. 189-91.
16. a) Jerry Bergman, "Vestigial Organs: Putative Evidence for Evolution of Homo Sapiens" (Unpublished Manuscript, 1306 North Orleans Ave., Bowling Green, Ohio 43402: 137 pages, 1984).
17. a) E. Lendell Cockrum and William J. McCauley, *Zoology* (W. B. Saunders Company, 1965), p. 163.
   b) Lynn Margulis and Karlene V. Schwartz, *Five Kingdoms: An Illustrated Guide to the Phyla of Life on Earth* (San Francisco: W. H. Freeman and Company, 1982). pp. 178-79.
   c) Actually, the form of life that has just over 20 cells is a very simple *parasite* called the mesozoa. It must have a complex animal as a host in order to provide it with such functions as digestion and respiration. The mesozoa could not be the evolutionary predecessors of any so-called higher animals since it requires a higher animal as its host. Sponges, the next most complex form of multicellular life, are so different from higher forms of life that even evolutionists do not consider them as ancestral to anything. (For example see Cockrum, above, p. 167.)
18. a) "This generalization was originally called the biogenic law by

Haeckel and is often stated as 'ontogeny recapitulates phylogeny.' This crude interpretation of embryological sequences will not stand close examination, however. Its shortcomings have been almost universally pointed out by modern authors, but the idea still has a prominent place in biological mythology."
>Paul R. Ehrlich and Richard W. Holm
>*The Process of Evolution* (New York: McGraw-Hill, 1963), p. 66.

b) "It is now firmly established that ontogeny does *not* repeat phylogeny." [emphasis theirs]
>George Gaylord Simpson and William Beck
>*Life: An Introduction to Biology* (New York: Harcourt, Brace and World, 1965), p. 241.

c) Hitching, pp. 202-5.

d) "The enthusiasm of the German zoologist, Ernst Haeckel, however, led to an erroneous and unfortunate exaggeration of the information which embryology could provide. This was known as the 'biogenic law' and claimed that embryology was a recapitulation of evolution, or that during its embryonic development an animal recapitulated the evolutionary history of its species."
>Sir Gavin R. de Beer
>(formerly Professor of Embryology in the University of London and Director of the British Museum of Natural History), *An Atlas of Evolution* (New York: Nelson, 1964), p. 38.

e) "... the theory of recapitulation has had a great and, while it lasted, regretable influence on the progress of embryology."
>Sir Gavin R. de Beer
>*Embryos and Ancestors* (London: Oxford University Press, 1951), p. 10.

f) "The biogenic law has become so deeply rooted in biological thought that it cannot be weeded out in spite of its having been demonstrated to be wrong by numerous subsequent scholars."
>Walter J. Bock
>Department of Biological Sciences, Columbia University, "Evolution by Orderly Law," *Science*, Vol. 164, 9 May 1969, pp. 684-685.

g) "... we no longer believe we can simply read in the embryonic development of a species its exact evolutionary history."
>Hurbert Frings and Marie Frings
>*Concepts of Zoology* (Toronto: Macmillan, 1970), p. 267.

h) "The type of analogical thinking which leads to theories that development is based on the recapitulation of ancestral stages or the like no longer seems at all convincing or even interesting to biologists."

Conrad Hal Waddington
Principles of Embryology (George Allen and Unwin, 1956), p. 10.

i) Haeckel, who in 1868 advanced this "Biogenic Law" that was quickly adopted in textbooks and encyclopedias throughout the world, distorted his data. Thompson explains:
"A natural law can only be established as an induction from facts. Haeckel was of course unable to do this. What he did was to arrange existing forms of animal life in a series proceeding from the simple to the complex, intercalating imaginary entities where discontinuity existed and then giving the embryonic phases names corresponding to the stages in his so-called evolutionary series. Cases in which this parallelism did not exist were dealt with by the simple expedient of saying that the embryological development had been falsified. When the 'convergence' of embryos was not entirely satisfactory, Haeckel altered the illustrations to fit his theory. The alterations were slight but significant. The 'biogenetic law' as a proof of evolution is valueless."
W. R. Thompson
"Introduction to *The Origin of Species*," by Charles Darwin; Everyman Library No. 811 (New York: E. P. Dutton & Sons, 1956 reprint of 1928 edition), p. 12.

j) M. Bowden, *Ape-Men: Fact or Fallacy?*, 2nd edition (Great Britain: Sovereign Publications, 1981), pp. 142-43.

k) Wilbert H. Rusch, Sr., "Ontogeny Recapitulates Phylogeny," *Creation Research Society Quarterly*, June 1969, pp. 27-34.

l) "To support his case he [Haeckel] began to fake evidence. Charged with fraud by five professors and convicted by a university court at Jena, he agreed that a small percentage of his embryonic drawings were forgeries; he was merely filling in and reconstructing the missing links when the evidence was thin, and he claimed unblushingly that 'hundreds of the best observers and biologists lie under the same charge.'"
Pitman, p. 120.

m) "... ontogeny recapitulates phylogeny, meaning that in the course of its development an embryo recapitulates the evolutionary history of its species. This idea was fathered by Ernst Haeckel, a German biologist who was so convinced that he had solved the riddle of life's unfolding that he doctored and faked his drawings of embryonic stages to prove his point."
Fix, p. 285.

19. a) M. Bowden, *Ape-Men: Fact or Fallacy?*, 2nd edition (Great Britain: Sovereign Publications, 1981).

b) Duane T. Gish, "Multivariate Analysis: Man ... Apes ... Australopithecines ...," *Battle for Creation* (San Diego: Creation Life Pub-

lishers, 1976), pp. 298-305.
c) Duane T. Gish, "Richard Leakey's Skull," *Battle for Creation* (San Diego: Creation Life Publishers, 1976), pp. 193-200.
d) Stephen J. Gould, "The Piltdown Conspiracy," *Natural History*, Vol. 89, No. 8, August 1980, pp. 8-28.
e) Allen L. Hammond, "Tales of an Elusive Ancestor," *Science 83*, November 1983, p. 43.
f) Adrienne L. Zihlman and J. Lowenstein, "False Start of the Human Parade," *Natural History*, Aug./Sept. 1979, pp. 86-91.
g) Hammond, p. 43.
h) "Pithecanthropus [Java man] was not a man, but a gigantic genus allied to the Gibbons, . . .
"... [Java Man had] a close affinity with the gibbon group of anthropoid apes.
"... This comparison more than confirms the opinion of Marcellin Boule, pronounced fifteen years ago, that Pithecanthropus may have been a large gibbonoid species, . . . "
    Euguene Dubois (the discoverer of Java man)
    "On the Fossil Human Skulls Recently Discovered in Java and Pithecanthropus Erectus," *Man*, January 1937, pp. 1-7.
i) C. L. Brace and Ashley Montagu, *Human Evolution*, 2nd edition (New York: Macmillan Publishing Co., Inc., 1977), p. 204.
j) Bowden, pp. 138-42, 144-48.
k) Hitching, pp. 208-9.
l) "The success of Darwinism was accompanied by a decline in scientific integrity . . . A striking example, which has only recently come to light, is the alteration of the Piltdown skull so that it could be used as evidence for the descent of man from the apes; but even before this a similar instance of tinkering with evidence was finally revealed by the discoverer of Pithecanthropus [Java man], who admitted, many years after his sensational report, that he had found in the same deposits bones that are definitely human."
    W. R. Thompson
    "Introduction to *The Origin of Species*," by Charles Darwin; Everyman No. 811 Library (New York: E. P. Dutton & Sons, 1956 reprint of 1928 edition), p. 17.
m) Patrick O'Connell, *Science of Today and the Problems of Genesis*, 2nd edition, 1969, pp. 139-42.
n) O'Connell, pp. 108-38.
o) Bowden, pp. 90-137.
p) "Either we toss out this skull or we toss out our theories of early man."
    Richard E. Leakey
    "Skull 1470—New Clue to Earliest Man?"
    National Geographic, June 1973, p. 819.

q) William R. Fix, *The Bone Peddlers: Selling Evolution* (New York: Macmillan, 1984), pp. 50-61.
r-t) Drs. Charles Oxnard and Solly Zuckerman, referred to below, were leaders in the development of a powerful multivariate analysis technique. This computerized technique simultaneously performs millions of comparisons on hundreds of corresponding dimensions of the bones of apes, humans, and the australopithecines. Their verdict, that the australopithecines are not intermediate between man and apes, is quite different from that of the more subjective and less analytical visual techniques of most anthropologists. This technique, however, has not yet been applied to the most recent type of australopithecine, commonly known as "Lucy."
r) "Let us now return to our original problem: the australopithecine fossils. I shall not burden you with details of each and every study that we have made, but table 1 summarizes the information and shows that whereas the conventional wisdom is that the australopithecine fragments are generally rather similar to humans and when different deviate somewhat towards the condition in the African apes, the new studies point to different conclusions. The new investigations suggest that the fossil fragments are usually uniquely different from any living form;"

  Charles E. Oxnard (Dean of the Graduate School, University of Southern California, Los Angeles, and from 1973-1978 a Dean at the University of Chicago), "Human Fossils: New Views of Old Bones," *The American Biology Teacher*, May 1979, p. 273.

s) Charles E. Oxnard, "The Place of the Australopithecines in Human Evolution: Grounds for Doubt?", *Nature*, Vol. 258, 4 December 1975, pp. 389-95.

t) "For my own part, the anatomical basis for the claim that the Australopithecines walked and ran upright like man is so much more flimsy than the evidence which points to the conclusion that their gait was some variant of what one sees in subhuman Primates, that it remains unacceptable."

  Sir Solly Zuckerman (former Chief Scientific Advisor to the British Government and Honorary Secretary of the Zoological Society of London), *Beyond the Ivory Tower* (New York: Taplinger Publishing Company, 1970), p. 93.

u) William L. Jungers, "Lucy's Limbs: Skeletal Allometry and Locomotion in Australopithecus Afarensis," *Nature*, 24 June 1982, pp. 676-78.

v) Jeremy Cherfas, "Trees Have Made Man Upright," *New Scientist*, 20 January 1983, pp. 172-78.

w) Jack T. Stern, Jr. and Randall L. Susman, "The Locomotor Anatomy of Australopithecus Afarensis," *American Journal of Physical*

Anthropology, Vol. 60, March 1983, pp. 279-317.
- x) Bowden, pp. 171-73.
- y) Francis Ivanhoe, "Was Virchow Right About Neanderthal?", *Nature*, Vol. 227, 8 August 1970, pp. 577-78.
- z) William L. Straus, Jr., and A. J. E. Cave, "Pathology and the Posture of Neanderthal Man," *The Quarterly Review of Biology*, December 1957, pp. 348-63.
- a1) Boyce Rensberger, "Facing the Past," *Science 81*, October 1981, p. 49.
- b1) See for example items 55-87.
20. a) Preston Cloud and Martin F. Glaessner, "The Ediacarian Period and System: Metazoa Inherit the Earth," *Science*, 27 August 1982, pp. 783-92, cover.
- b) Martin F. Glaessner, "Pre-Cambrian Animals," *Scientific American*, Vol. 24, No. 3, pp. 72-78.
- c) Donald G. Mikulic, et al., "A Silurian Soft-Bodied Biota," *Science*, Vol. 228, 10 May 1985, pp. 715-17.
- d) A. Snelling, J. Mackay, C. Wieland, and K. Ham, *The Case Against Evolution: The Case for Creation* (Australia: Creation Science Foundation, 1983), p. 10.
21. a) J. D. Whitney, "The Auriferous Gravels of the Sierra Nevada of California," *Memoirs of the Museum of Comparative Zoology of Harvard College*, Vol. VI, 1880, pp. 258-88.
- b) Bowden, pp. 76-78.
- c) Frank W. Cousins, *Fossil Man* (Emsworth, England: A. E. Norris & Sons Ltd., 1971), pp. 50-52, 82, 83.
- d) William H. Holmes, "Review of the Evidence Relating to Auriferous Gravel Man in California," *Smithsonian Institutional Annual Report*, 1899, pp. 419-72.
- e) W. H. B., "Alleged Discovery of An Ancient Human Skull in California," *American Journal of Science*, Vol. 2, 1866, p. 424.
- f) Bowden, pp. 78-79.
- g) Cousins, pp. 48-50, 81.
- h) Bowden, pp. 183-93.
- i) Bowden, pp. 79-88.
- j) William L. Straus, Jr., "A New Oreopithecus Skeleton," *Science*, Vol. 128, 5 September 1958, p. 523.
- k) William L. Straus, Jr., "Oreopithecus Bambolii," *Science*, Vol. 126, 23 August 1957, pp. 345-46.
- l) F. A. Barnes, "The Case of the Bones in Stone," *Desert Magazine*, Vol. 38, February 1975, pp. 36-39.
- m) Clifford L. Burdick, "Discovery of Human Skeletons in Cretaceous Formation," *Creation Research Society Quarterly*, September 1973, pp. 109-10.
- n) Fix, pp. 98-105.
- o) J. B. Birdsell, *Human Evolution* (Chicago: Rand McNally, 1972), pp. 316-18.

22. a) "... by this theory innumerable transitional forms must have existed, why do we not find them imbedded in countless numbers in the crust of the earth?"
Charles Darwin
The Origin of Species, 6th edition (New York: Macmillan, 1927), p. 163.
"... the number of intermediate varieties, which have formerly existed [must] truly be enormous. Why then is not every geological formation and every stratum full of such intermediate links? Geology assuredly does not reveal any such finely-graduated organic chain; and this, perhaps, is the most obvious and serious objection which can be urged against this theory."
Darwin, p. 323.
b) Dr. Colin Patterson, a senior paleontologist at the British Museum of Natural History, was asked by Luther D. Sunderland why no evolutionary transitions were included in Dr. Patterson's recent book entitled *Evolution*. In a personal letter dated April 10, 1979, Patterson said:
"I fully agree with your comments on the lack of direct illustration of evolutionary transitions in my book. If I knew of any, fossil or living, I would certainly have included them. You suggest that an artist should be asked to visualise such transformations, but where would he get the information from? I could not, honestly, provide it, and if I were to leave it to artistic license, would that not mislead the reader?... Yet Gould and the American Museum people are hard to contradict when they say that there are no transitional fossils. As a palaeontologist myself, I am much occupied with the philosophical problems of identifying ancestral forms in the fossil record. You say that I should at least 'show a photo of the fossil from which each type organism was derived.' I will lay it on the line—there is not one such fossil for which one could make a watertight argument."
c) "When you look for links between major groups of animals, they simply aren't there; at least, not in enough numbers to put their status beyond doubt. Either they don't exist at all, or they are so rare that endless argument goes on about whether a particular fossil is, or isn't, or might be, transitional between this group or that."
Hitching, p. 19.
d) "The smooth transition from one form of life to another which is implied in the theory is ... not borne out by the facts. The search for 'missing links' between various living creatures, like humans and apes, is probably fruitless ... because they probably never existed as distinct transitional types ... But no one has yet found any evidence of such transitional creatures. This oddity has been attributed to gaps in the fossil record which gradualists expected to

fill when rock strata of the proper age had been found. In the last decade, however, geologists have found rock layers of all divisions of the last 500 million years and no transitional forms were contained in them. If it is not the fossil record which is incomplete then it must be the theory."
    Niles Eldredge (Invertebrate Paleontologist)
    American Museum of Natural History, *Guardian*, 21 November 1978.

e) "There is no more conclusive refutation of Darwinism than that furnished by palaeontology. Simple probability indicates that fossil hoards can only be test samples. Each sample, then, should represent a different stage of evolution, and there ought to be merely 'transitional' types, no definition and no species. Instead of this we find perfectly stable and unaltered forms persevering through long ages, forms that have not developed themselves on the fitness principle, but *appear suddenly and at once in their definitive shape*; that do not thereafter evolve towards better adaptation, but become rarer and finally disappear, while quite different forms crop up again. What unfolds itself, in ever-increasing richness of form, is the great classes and kinds of living beings which exist aboriginally and *exist still, without transition types*, in the groupings of today." [emphasis his]
    Oswald Spengler
    The Decline of the West, Vol. 2 (New York: Alfred A. Knopf, 1914), p. 32.

f) "This regular absence of transitional forms is not confined to mammals, but is an almost universal phenomenon, as has long been noted by paleontologists. It is true of almost all orders of all classes of animals, both vertebrate and invetebrate. A fortiori, it is also true of the classes, themselves, and of the major animal phyla, and it is apparently also true of analogous categories of plants."
    George Gaylord Simpson
    Tempo and Mode in Evolution (New York: Columbia University Press, 1944), p. 106.

g) The Field Museum of Natural History in Chicago has one of the largest collections of fossils in the world. Consequently, its Dean, Dr. David Raup, was eminently qualified to summarize the situation regarding the transitions that should be observed in the fossil record.
"Well, we are now about 120 years after Darwin and the knowledge of the fossil record has been greatly expanded. We now have a quarter of a million fossil species but the situation hasn't changed much. The record of evolution is still surprisingly jerky and, ironically, we have fewer examples of evolutionary transition than we had in Darwin's time. By this I mean that some of the classic cases of darwinian change in the fossil record, such as the evolution of

the horse in North America, have had to be discarded or modified as a result of more detailed information—what appeared to be a nice simple progression when relatively few data were available now appears to be much less gradualistic. So Darwin's problem has not been alleviated in the last 120 years and we still have a record which does show change but one that can hardly be looked upon as the most reasonable consequence of natural selection."
    David M. Raup (Dean of the Field Museum of Natural History), "Conflicts Between Darwin and Paleontology," *Field Museum of Natural History Bulletin*, January 1979, p. 25.

h) "... there are about 25 major living subdivisions (phyla) of the animal kingdom alone, all with gaps between them that are not bridged by known intermediates.

"Most orders, classes, and phyla appear abruptly [in the fossil record], and commonly have already acquired all the characters that distinguish them."
    Francisco J. Ayala and James W. Valentine
    Evolving, The Theory and Processes of Organic Evolution, 1979, pp. 258, 266-67.

i) "All paleontologists know that the fossil record contains precious little in the way of intermediate forms; transitions between major groups are characteristically abrupt."
    Stephen J. Gould
    "The Return of Hopeful Monsters," *Natural History*, Vol. 86, June 1977, pp. 22-30.

j) "... the geologic record did not then and still does not yield a finely graduated chain of slow and progressive evolution. In other words, there are not enough intermediates. There are very few cases where one can find a gradual transition from one species to another and very few cases where one can look at a part of the fossil record and actually see that organisms were improving in the sense of becoming better adapted."
    David M. Raup
    "Conflicts Between Darwin and Paleontology," *Field Museum of Natural History Bulletin*, January 1979, p. 23.

k) "The extreme rarity of transitional forms in the fossil record persists as the trade secret of paleontology. The evolutionary trees that adorn our textbooks have data only at the tips and nodes of their branches; the rest is inference, however reasonable, not the evidence of fossils."
    Stephen Jay Gould
    "Evolution's Erratic Pace," *Natural History*, Vol. 5, May 1977, p. 14.

l) "... the gradual morphological transitions between presumed ancestors and descendants, anticipated by most biologists, are missing."
   David E. Schindel (Curator of Invertebrate Fossils, Peabody Museum of Natural History), "The Gaps in the Fossil Record," *Nature*, Vol. 297, 27 May 1982, pp. 282-84.

m) "Despite the bright promise that paleontology provides a means of 'seeing' evolution, it has presented some nasty difficulties for evolutionists the most notorious of which is the presence of 'gaps' in the fossil record. Evolution requires intermediate forms between species and paleontology does not provide them."
   David B. Kitts (School of Geology and Geophysics, University of Oklahoma), "Paleontology and Evolutionary Theory," *Evolution*, Vol. 28, September 1974, p. 467.

n) "In spite of the immense amount of the paleontological material and the existence of long series of intact stratigraphic sequences with perfect records for the lower categories, transitions between the higher categories are missing."
   Richard B. Goldschmidt
   "Evolution, As Viewed by One Geneticist," *American Scientist*, Vol. 40, January 1952, p. 98.

o) "There are no intermediate forms between finned and limbed creatures in the fossil collections of the world."
   Gordon Rattray Taylor
   The Great Evolution Mystery (New York: Harper & Row, 1983), p. 60.

p) "The origin of birds is largely a matter of deduction. There is no fossil evidence of the stages through which the remarkable change from reptile to bird was achieved."
   W. E. Swinton
   "The Origin of Birds," in *Biology and Comparative Physiology of Birds*, edited by A. J. Marshall (Academic Press, 1960), Vol. 1, Chapter 1, p. 1.

q) Some people claim that Archaeopteryx is a transition between the reptiles and birds. Of the relatively few alleged transitional fossils, this is probably the most frequently cited. Recently however, several very prominent scientists have charged that a forgery has occurred. A strong case can be made that on the two Archaeopteryx specimens where feathers are clearly visible, it appears that the imprint of the feather was added after the fossils were discovered. For the many details see:
   q1) Moshe Trop, "Is the Archaeopteryx a Fake?", *Creation Research Society Quarterly*, Vol. 20, No. 2, September 1983, pp. 121-22.
   q2) R. S. Watkins, F. Hoyle, N. C. Wickramasinghe, J. Watkins, R. Rabilizirov, and L. M. Spetner, "Archaeopteryx: A Photo-

graphic Study," *The British Journal of Photography*, Vol. 132, 8 March 1985, pp. 264-66.
q3) R. S. Watking, F. Hoyle, N. C. Wickramasinghe, J. Watkins, R. Rabilizirov, and L. M. Spetner, "Archaeopteryx: A Further Comment," *The British Journal of Photography*, Vol. 132, 28 March 1985, pp. 358ff.
q4) R. S. Watkins, F. Hoyle, N. C. Wickramasinghe, J. Watkins, R. Rabilizirov, and L. M. Spetner, "Archaeopteryx: Further Evidence," *The British Journal of Photography*, Vol. 132, 26 April 1985, pp. 468-70.
q5) F. Hoyle, N. C. Wickramasinghe, and R. S. Watkins, "Archaeopteryx," *The British Journal of Photography*, Vol. 132, 21 June 1985, pp. 693-703.

r) "It may, therefore, be firmly maintained that it is not even possible to make a caricature of an evolution out of palaeobiological facts. The fossil material is now so complete that it has been possible to construct new classes and the lack of transitional series cannot be explained as due to the scarcity of the material. The deficiencies are real, they will never be filled."
    N. Heribert Nilsson of Lund University
    Synthetische Artbildung (Lund Sweden: Verlag CWK Gleerup, 1953), p. 1212.

s) "One of the major unsolved problems of geology and evolution is the occurrence of diversified, multicellular marine invertebrates in Lower Cambrian rocks on all the continents and their absence in rocks of greater age."
    Daniel I. Axelrod
    "Early Cambrian Marine Fauna," *Science*, 4 July 1958, p. 7.

t) "But whatever ideas authorities may have on the subject, lungfishes, like every othr major group of fishes that I know, have their origins firmly based in *nothing* . . ."
    Errol White
    "A Little on Lung-fishes," *Proceedings of the Linnean Society of London*, Vol. 177, Presidential Address, January 1966, p. 8.

u) Cloud and Glaessner, pp. 783-92.

v) A. K. Ghosh and A. Bose, "Occurrence of Microflora in the Salt Pseudomorph Beds, Salt Range, Punjab," *Nature*, Vol. 160, 6 December 1947, pp. 796-97.

w) J. Coates, *et al.*, "Age of the Saline Series in the Punjab Salt Range," *Nature*, Vol. 155, 3 March 1945, pp. 266-67.

x) John E. Repetski, "A Fish from the Upper Cambrian of North America," *Science*, Vol. 200, 5 May 1978, pp. 529-31.

y) Peter Farb, *Life Nature Library: The Insects* (New York: Time Incorporated, 1962), p. 14.

23. a) Walter E. Lammerts has published three lists documenting 69 wrong-order formations, just in the United States: "Recorded Instances of Wrong-Order Formations or Presumed Overthrusts in the United States: Parts I-III," *Creation Research Society Quarterly*, Vol. 21, September 1984, p. 88, December 1984, p. 150, and March 1985, p. 200.
    b) A. K. Ghosh and A. Bose, p. 796-97.
    c) A. K. Ghosh and A. Bose, "Spores and Tracheids from the Cambrian of Kashmir," *Nature*, Vol. 169, 21 June, pp. 1056-57.
    d) J. Coates *et al.*, pp. 266-67.
    e) Yu. Kruzhilin and V. Ovcharov, "A Horse from the Dinosaur Epoch?", *Moskovskaya Pravda* (Moscow Truth), 5 February 1984.
    f) Cr. V. Rubstov, "Tracking Dinosaurs," *Moscow News*, No. 24, p. 10, 1983.
    g) Andrew Snelling, "Fossil Bluff," *Ex Nihilo*, Vol. 7, No. 3, March 1985, p. 8.
25. a) Duane T. Gish, Speculations and Experiments Related to Theories on the Origin of Life, ICR Technical Monograph No. 1 (El Cajon, CA: Institute for Creation Research, 1972).
    b) Hitching, p. 65.
26. a) Charles F. Davidson, "Geochemical Aspects of Atmospheric Evolution," *Proceedings of the National Academy of Sciences*, Vol. 53, 15 June 1965, pp. 1194-1205.
    b) Steven A. Austin, "Did the Early Earth Have a Reducing Atmosphere?," *ICR Impact*, No. 109, July 1982.
    c) "In general, we find no evidence in the sedimentary distributions of carbon, sulfur, uranium, or iron, that an oxygen-free atmosphere has existed at any time during the span of geological history recorded in well preserved sedimentary rocks."
        Erich Dimroth and Michael M. Kimberly
        "Precambrian Atmospheric Oxygen: Evidence in the Sedimentary Distributions of Carbon, Sulfur, Uranium, and Iron," *Canadian Journal of Earth Sciences*, Vol. 13, No. 9, September 1976, p. 1161.
    d) "I believe this [the overwhelming tendency for chemical reactions to move in the direction opposite to that required for the evolution of life] to be the most stubborn problem that confronts us—the weakest link at present in our argument [for the origin of life]."
        George Wald
        "The Origin of Life," *Scientific American*, Vol. 190, August 1954, p. 50.
    e) "The conclusion from these arguments presents the most serious obstacle, if indeed it is not fatal, to the theory of spontaneous generation. First, thermodynamic calculations predict vanishingly small concentrations of even the simplest organic com-

pounds. Secondly, the reactions that are invoked to synthesize such compounds are seen to be much more effective in decomposing them."
  D. E. Hull
  "Thermodynamics and Kinetics of Spontaneous Generation," *Nature*, Vol. 186, 28 May 1960, p. 694.
 f) Pitman, p. 140.
 g) Gish, *Speculations and Experiments Related to Theories on the Origin of Life*.
 h) Duane T. Gish, "Gish Debates Russell Doolittle at Iowa State," *Acts and Facts*, Vol. 9, No. 12, December 1980, p. 2.
27. a) Experts in this field hardly ever discuss this matter publicly. However, the leading evolutionists in the world know that this problem exists. For example, in an approved transcript of a taped interview with Dr. David Raup of the Field Museum of Natural History in Chicago, Luther D. Sutherland commented to Dr. Raup that "Neither Dr. Patterson [of the British Museum of Natural History] nor Dr. Eldredge [of the American Museum of Natural History] could give me any explanation of the origination of the first cell." Dr. Raup replied, "I can't either."
28. Similar problems have been acknowledged by several prominent writers.
 a) "But then arises the doubt, can the mind of man, which has, as I fully believe, been developed from a mind as low as that possessed by the lowest animals, be trusted when it draws such grand conclusions? I cannot pretend to throw the least light on such abstruse problems."
  Charles Darwin
  The Life and Letters of Charles Darwin, edited by Francis Darwin, (London: John Murray, 1888), Vol. 1, p. 313.
 b) "For if my mental processes are determined wholly by the motions of atoms in my brain, I have no reason to suppose that my beliefs are true. They may be sound chemically, but that does not make them sound logically. And hence I have no reason for supposing my brain to be composed of atoms."
  Professor J.B.S. Haldane
  Possible Worlds (London: Chatto & Windus, 1927), p. 209.
 c) "If the solar system was brought about by an accidental collision, then the appearance of organic life on this planet was also an accident, and the whole evolution of Man was an accident too. If so, then all our present thoughts are mere accidents—the accidental by-product of the movement of atoms. And this holds for the thoughts of the materialists and astronomers as well as for anyone else's. But if their thoughts—i.e. of Materialism and Astronomy—are merely accidental by-products, why should we believe them to

be true? I see no reason for believing that one accident should be able to give me a correct account of all the other accidents."
C.S. Lewis
God In the Dock (Eerdmans Publishing Company, 1970), pp. 52-53.
29. a) Dr. Colin Patterson is the Senior Principal Scientific Officer in the Palaeontology Department at the British Museum of Natural History. In a talk he gave on November 5, 1981 to leading evolutionists at the American Museum of Natural History, he presented some new data on amino acid sequences in several proteins of a number of animals. The relationships of these animals, according to evolutionary theory, has been taught in classrooms for many decades. Dr. Patterson pointed out to a stunned audience that this new data contradicts the theory of evolution. In his words, "The theory makes a prediction; we've tested it, and the prediction is falsified precisely." Although he acknowledged that scientific falsification is never absolute, the thrust of his entire talk was that he now realized that "evolution was a faith," that he had "been duped into taking evolution as revealed truth in some way," and "that evolution not only conveys no knowledge but seems to convey anti-knowledge, apparent knowledge which is harmful to systematics [the science of classifying different forms of life]."
"Prominent British Scientist Challenges Evolution Theory," Audio Tape Transcription and Summary by Luther D. Sunderland, 5 Griffin Drive, Apalachin, New York 13732.
  b) Michael Denton, *Evolution: A Theory in Crisis* (London: Burnett Books, 1985), p. 285.
  c) "The really significant finding that comes to light from comparing the proteins' amino acid sequences is that it is impossible to arrange them in any sort of evolutionary series."
Denton, p. 289.
"In terms of their biochemistry, none of the species deemed 'intermediate,' 'ancestral' or 'primitive' by generations of evolutionary biologists, and alluded to as evidence of sequence in nature, show any sign of their supposed intermediate status."
Denton, p. 293.
  d) Ginny Gray, "Student Project 'Rattles' Science Fair Judges," *Issues and Answers*, December 1980, p. 3.
  e) Robert Bayne Brown, *Abstracts: 31st International Science and Engineering Fair* (Washington D.C.: Science Service, 1980), p. 113.
33. a) Carl Sagan, *The Dragons of Eden* (New York: Random House, 1977), p. 25.
  b) "Biochemical systems are exceedingly complex, so much so that the chance of their being formed through random shufflings of

simple organic molecules is exceedingly minute, to a point indeed where it is insensibly different from zero."

    Sir Fred Hoyle and N. Chandra Wickramasinghe
    Evolution from Space (New York: Simon and Schuster, 1981), p. 3.

"No matter how large the environment one considers, life cannot have had a random beginning. Troops of monkeys thundering away at random on typewriters could not produce the works of Shakespeare, for the practical reason that the whole observable universe is not large enough to contain the necessary monkey hordes, the necessary typewriters, and certainly the waste paper baskets required for the deposition of wrong attempts. The same is true for living material."

    Hoyle and Wickramasinghe, p. 148.

"The trouble is that there are about two thousand enzymes, and the chance of obtaining them all in a random trial is only one part in $(10^{20})^{2000} = 10^{40000}$, an outrageously small probability that could not be faced even if the whole universe consisted of organic soup.

"If one is not prejudiced either by social beliefs or by a scientific training into the conviction that life originated on the Earth, this simple calculation wipes the idea entirely out of court."

    Hoyle and Wickramasinghe, p. 24.

"From the beginning of this book we have emphasized the enormous information content of even the simplest living systems. The information cannot in our view be generated by what are often called 'natural' processes, as for instance through meteorological and chemical processes occurring at the surface of a lifeless planet. As well as a suitable physical and chemical environment, a large initial store of information was also needed. We have argued that the requisite information came from an 'intelligence,' the beckoning spectre."

    Hoyle and Wickramasinghe, p. 150.

c) Murry Eden, as reported in "Heresy in the Halls of Biology: Mathematicians Question Darwinism," *Scientific Research*, November 1967, p. 64.

d) "It is our contention that if 'random' is given a serious and crucial interpretation from a probabilistic point of view, the randomness postulate is highly implausible and that an adequate scientific theory of evolution must await the discovery and elucidation of new natural laws—physical, physico-chemical, and biological."

    Murray Eden
    Mathematical Challenges to the Neo-Darwinian Interpretation of Evolution, Paul S. Moorhead and Martin M. Kaplan, editors, proceedings of a symposium held at the Wistar Institute of Anatomy and Biology, April 25 and 26,

1966 (Philadelphia: The Wistar Institute Press, 1967), p. 109.
31. a) Richard E. Dickerson, "Chemical Evolution and the Origin of Life," *Scientific American*, Vol. 239, September 1978, p. 73.
    b) Hitching, p. 66.
    c) "The origin of the genetic code presents formidable unsolved problems. The coded information in the nucleotide sequence is meaningless without the transition machinery, but the specification for this machinery is itself coded in the DNA. Thus without the machinery the information is meaningless, but without the coded information the machinery cannot be produced! This presents a paradox of the 'chicken and egg' variety, and attempts to solve it have so far been sterile."
    John C. Walton
    (Lecturer in Chemistry, University of St. Andrews Fife, Scotland), "Organization and the Origin of Life," *Origins*, Vol. 4, No. 1, 1977, pp. 30-31.
32. a) James F. Coppedge, *Evolution: Possible or Impossible?* (Grand Rapids: Zondervan Publishing House, 1973), pp. 71-79.
    b) A. E. Wilder Smith, *The Natural Sciences Know Nothing of Evolution* (San Diego: Master Books, 1980), pp. 15-32, 154-160.
33. a) Coppedge, pp. 71-72.
    b) "Whether one looks to mutations or gene flow for the sourse of the variations needed to fuel evolution, there is an enormous probability problem at the core of Darwinist and neo-Darwinist theory, which has been cited by hundreds of scientists and professionals. Engineers, physicists, astronomers, and biologists who have looked without prejudice at the notion of such variations producing ever more complex organisms have come to the same conclusion: The evolutionists are assuming the impossible.
    "Even if we take the simplest large protein molecule that can reproduce itself if immersed in a bath of nutrients, the odds against this developing by chance range from one in 10^{450} (engineer Marcel Goulay in *Analytical Chemistry*) to one in 10^{600} (Frank Salisbury in *American Biology Teacher*).
    William R. Rix, p. 196.
34. a) Oscar L. Brauer, "The Smyrna Fig Requires God for Its Production," *Creation Research Society Quarterly*, Vol. 9, No. 2, September 1972, pp. 129-31.
    b) Bob Devine, *Mr. Baggy-Skin Lizard* (Chicago: Moody Press, 1977), pp. 29-32.
    c) These and other problems are recognized by leading evolutionists.
    a) "This book is written from a conviction that the prevalence of sexual reproduction in higher plants and animals is inconsistent with current evolutionary theory."
    George C. Williams

Preface, *Sex and Evolution* (Princeton, N.J.: Princeton University Press, 1975), p. v.

b) "Indeed, the persistence of sex is one of the fundamental mysteries in evolutionary biology today."

Gina Maranto and Shannon Brownlee
"Why Sex?", *Discover*, February 1984, pp. 24-28.

c) "So why is there sex? We do not have a compelling answer to the question. Despite some ingenious suggestions by orthodox Darwinians (notably G. C. Williams 1975; John Maynard Smith 1978), there is no convincing Darwinian history for the emergence of sexual reproduction. However, evolutionary theorists believe that the problem will be solved without abandoning the main Darwinian insights—just as early nineteenth-century astronomers believed that the problem of the motion of Uranus could be overcome without major modification of Newton's celestial mechanics."

Philip Kitcher
Abusing Science: The Case Against Creationism (Cambridge, Massachusetts: The MIT Press, 1982), p. 54.

d) "From an evolutionary viewpoint the sex differentiation is impossible to understand, as well as the structural sexual differences between the systematic categories which are sometimes immense. We know that intersexes within a species must be sterile. How is it, then, possible to imagine bridges between two amazingly different structural types."

N. Heribert Nilsson, p. 1225

36. a) "Ounce for ounce, watt for watt, it [the bat] is millions of times more efficient and more sensitive than the radars and sonars contrived by man."

Pitman, p. 219

b) Robert E. Kofahl and Kelly L. Seagraves, *The Creation Explanation* (Wheaton, Illinois: Harold Shaw Publishers, 1975), pp. 2-9.

c) Thomas Eisner and Daniel J. Aneshansley, "Spray Aiming in Bombardier Beetles: Jet Deflection by the Coanda Effect," *Science*, Vol. 215, 1 January 1982, pp. 83-85.

37-41. a) "To sum up, I think that all suggested accounts of the origin of the Solar System are subject to serious objections. The conclusion in the present state of the subject would be that the system cannot exist."

Sir Harold Jeffreys
The Earth: Its Origin, History, and Physical Constitution, 6th edition (Cambridge England: Cambridge University Press, 1976), p. 387.

b) "But if we had a reliable theory of the origin of planets, if we knew of some mechanism consistent with the laws of physics so that we

understood how planets form, then clearly we could make use of it to estimate the probability that other stars have attendant planets. However, no such theory exists yet, despite the large number of hypotheses suggested."
  R. A. Lyttleton
  Mysteries of the Solar System, 6th edition (Oxford, England: Clarendon Press, 1968), p. 4.
 c) "A great array of observational facts must be explained by a satisfactory theory, [on the evolution of the solar system] and the theory must be consistent with the principles of dynamic and modern physics. All of the hypotheses so far presented have failed, or remain unproved, when physical theory is properly applied."
  Fred L. Whipple
  Earth, Moon, and Planets (Cambridge, Massachusetts: Harvard University Press, 1970), p. 243.
37. d) *The Astronomical Almanac for the Year 1985* (Washington, D.C.: U.S. Government Printing Office, 1985), p. E88.
38. d) *The Astronomical Almanac*, p. F2.
39. d) *The Astronomical Almanac*, p. F2.
40. d) *Van Nostrand's Scientific Encyclopedia* (Van Nostrand Reinhold Co., 5th edition, 1976), pp. 493-94.
 e) "First, we see that material torn from the Sun would not be at all suitable for the formation of the planets as we know them. Its composition would be hopelessly wrong. And our second point in this contrast is that it is the Sun that is normal and the Earth that is the freak. The interstellar gas and most of the stars are composed of material like the Sun, not like the earth. You must understand that, cosmically speaking, the room you are now sitting in is made of the wrong stuff. You, yourself, are a rarity. You are a cosmic collector's piece."
  Fred Hoyle
  "The Nature of the Universe," Part IV, *Harper's Magazine*, March 1951, p. 65.
41. d) R. A. Lyttleton, *Mysteries of the Solar System*, 6th edition (Oxford, England: Clarendon Press, 1968), p. 16.
 e) Fred Hoyle, *The Cosmology of the Solar System* (Enslow Publishers, 1979), pp. 11-12.
42. a) Paul M. Steidl, *The Earth, the Stars, and the Bible* (Grand Rapids: Baker Book House, 1979), p. 106.
44. a) "The whole subject of the origin of the moon must be regarded as highly speculative."
  Robert C. Haymes
  Introduction to Space Science (New York: John Wiley & Sons, Inc., 1971), p. 209.
 b) "Dr. Harold Urey, a Nobel prize-winning chemist and lunar sci-

entist, expresses his attitude: 'I do not know the origin of the moon. I'm not sure of my own or any other's models. I'd lay odds against any of the models proposed being correct."
John C. Whitcomb and Donald B. DeYoung
The Moon (Winona Lake, Indiana: BHM Books, 1978), p. 50.
c) Haymes, p. 209.
d) Steidl, pp. 77-79.
e) M. Mitchell Waldrop, "The Origin of the Moon," *Science*, Vol. 216, 7 May 1982, pp. 606-7.
f) Frank D. Stacey, *Physics of the Earth* (New York: John Wiley & Sons, Inc., 1969), pp. 38-39.
45. a) Nathan R. Wood, *The Secret of the Universe* (Grand Rapids: Eerdmans Publishing Co., 1936, 10th edition).
48. a) Sir Isaac Newton, source unknown.
50. a) H. P. Gush, "Rocket Measurement of the Cosmic Background Submillimeter Spectrum," *Physical Review Letters*, Vol. 47, No. 10, 7 September 1981, pp. 745-48.
b) Kandiah Shivanandan, James R. Houck, and Martin O. Harwit, "Preliminary Observations of the Far-Infrared Night-Sky Background Radiation," *Physical Review Letters*, 11 November 1968, Vol. 21, pp. 1460-62.
c) "Freak Result Verified," *Nature*, Vol. 223, 23 August 1969, pp. 779-80.
d) Steidl, pp. 207-8.
e) D. W. Sciama, *Modern Cosmology* (London: Cambridge University Press, 1971), pp. 149-55.
f) Geoffrey Burbridge, "Was There Really a Big Bang?" *Nature*, Vol. 233, 3 September 1971, pp. 36-40.
g) Ben Patrusky, "Why Is the Cosmos 'Lumpy'?" *Science 81*, June 1981, p. 96.
h) "Deep Redshift Survey of Galaxies Suggests Million-Mpc^3 Void," *Physics Today*, January 1982, Vol. 35, pp. 17-19.
i) Stephen A. Gregory and Laird A. Thompson, "Superclusters and Voids in the Distribution of Galaxies," *Scientific American*, March 1982, pp. 106-14.
51. a) Harwit, *Astrophysical Concepts* (New York: John C. Wiley, 1973), p. 394.
b) "... there is no reasonable astronomical scenario in which mineral grains can condense."
Sir Fred Hoyle and N. Chandra Wickramasinghe
"Where Microbes Boldly Went," *New Scientist*, 13 August 1981, p. 413.
52. a) Steidl, *The Earth, the Stars, and the Bible*, pp. 143-45.
53. a) Steidl, *The Earth, the Stars, and the Bible*, pp. 134-36.

54. a) "There is much doubt, however, that galaxies evolve from one type to another at all."
 George Abell
 Exploration of the Universe, 2nd edition (New York: Holt, Rinehart, and Winston, 1969), p. 629.
 b) "Our conclusions, then, are that the sequence of the classification of galaxies is not an evolutionary sequence..."
 Paul W. Hodge
 Galaxies and Cosmology (New York: McGraw-Hill Book Co., 1966), p. 122.
 c) Hodge, p. 123.
 d) Harold S. Slusher, "Clues Regarding the Age of the Universe," *ICR Impact*, No. 19 (El Cajon, California: Institute for Creation Research), pp. 2-3.
 e) Steidl, pp. 161-87.
56. a) Robert V. Gentry, "Radiohalos in Coalified Wood: New Evidence Relating to the Time of Uranium Introduction and Coalification," *Science*, Vol. 194, 15 October 1976, pp. 315-17.
 b) Robert V. Gentry, "On the Invariance of the Decay Constant Over Geological Time," *Creation Research Society Quarterly*, Vol. 5, September 1968, pp. 83-84.
57. a) John Woodmorappe, "Radiometric Geochronology Reappraised," *Creation Research Society Quarterly*, Vol. 16, September 1979, pp. 102-29.
 b) Robert H. Brown, "Graveyard Clock: Do They Really Tell Time?", *Signs of the Times*, June 1982, pp. 8-9.
58. a) Robert H. Brown, "Can We Believe Radiocarbon Dates?", *Creation Research Society Quarterly*, Vol. 12, No. 1, June 1975, pp. 66-68.
 b) Robert H. Brown, "Regression Analysis of C-14 Age Profiles," unpublished manuscript, 28 July 1980.
59. a) Robert V. Gentry, "'Spectacle' Array of 210Po Halo Radiocentres In Biotite: A Nuclear Geophysical Enigma," *Nature*, 13 December 1974, pp. 564-66.
 b) Robert V. Gentry, "Radiohalos In Radiochronological and Cosmological Perspective," *Science*, 5 April 1974, Vol. 184, pp. 62-66.
60. a) "It cannot be denied that from a strictly philosophical standpoint geologists are here arguing in a circle. The succession of organisms has been determined by a study of their remains embedded in the rocks, and the relative ages of the rocks are determined by the remains of organisms that they contain."
 R. H. Rastall
 "Geology," *Encyclopaedia Britannica*, 1954, Vol. 10, p. 168.
 b) "Are the authorities maintaining, on the one hand, that evolution is documented by geology and, on the other hand, that geology is

documented by evolution? Isn't this a circular argument?"
Larry Azar
"Biologists, Help!", *Bioscience*, Vol. 28, November 1978, p. 714.

c) "The intelligent layman has long suspected circular reasoning in the use of rocks to date fossils and fossils to date rocks. The geologist has never bothered to think of a good reply, feeling that explanations are not worth the trouble as long as the work brings results. This is supposed to be hard-headed pragmatism."
J. E. O'Rourke
"Pragmatism Versus Materialism in Stratigraphy," *American Journal of Science*, Vol. 276, January 1976, p. 47.

"The rocks do date the fossils, but the fossils date the rocks more accurately. Stratigraphy cannot avoid this kind of reasoning, if it insists on using only temporal concepts, because circularity is inherent in the derivation of time scales."
O'Rourke, p. 53.

Although O'Rourke attempts to justify current practices of stratigraphers, he recognizes the inherent problems associated with this circular reasoning.

d) "But the danger of circularity is still present. For most biologists the strongest reason for accepting the evolutionary hypothesis is their acceptance of some theory that entails it. There is another difficulty. The temporal ordering of biological events beyond the local section may critically involve paleontological correlation, which necessarily presupposes the non-repeatability of organic events in geologic history. There are various justifications for this assumption but for almost all contemporary paleontologists it rests upon the acceptance of the evolutionary hypothesis."
David B. Kitts
"Paleontology and Evolutionary Theory," *Evolution*, Vol. 28, September 1974, p. 466.

e) "It is a problem not easily solved by the classic methods of stratigraphical paleontology, as obviously we will land ourselves immediately in an impossible circular argument if we say, firstly that a particular lithology is synchronous on the evidence of its fossils, and secondly that the fossils are synchronous on the evidence of the lithology."
Derek V. Ager
The Nature of the Stratigraphical Record, 2nd edition (New York: John Wiley and Sons, Inc., 1981), p. 68.

f) See references for items 23 and 62.

61. a) "We are only kidding ourselves if we think that we have anything

like a complete succession for any part of the stratigraphical column in any one place."
Derek V. Ager, p. 32.
- b) John Woodmorappe, "The Essential Nonexistence of the Evolutionary-Uniformitarian Geologic Column: A Quantitative Assessment," *Creation Research Society Quarterly*, Vol. 18, No. 1, June 1981, pp. 46-71.
62. a) Ariel A. Roth, "Coral Reef Growth," *Origins*, Vol. 6, No. 2, 1979, pp. 88-95.
- b) Ian T. Taylor, *In the Minds of Men* (Toronto: TFE Publishing, 1984), pp. 335-36.
63. a) Rene Noorbergen, *Secrets of the Lost Races* (New York: The Bobbs-Merrill Company, Inc., 1977), pp. 40-62.
- b) Harry V. Wiant, Jr., "A Curiosity From Coal," *Creation Research Society Quarterly*, Vol. 13, No. 1, June 1976, p. 74.
- c) J. R. Jochmans, "Strange Relics from the Depths of the Earth," *Bible-Science Newsletter*, January 1979, p. 1.
- d) Wilbert H. Rusch, Sr., "Human Footprints in Rocks," *Creation Research Society Quarterly*, March 1971, pp. 201-2.
- e) Frederick G. Wright, "The Idaho Find," *American Antiquarian*, Vol. II, 1889, pp. 379-81, as cited by William R. Corliss in *Ancient Man, A Handbook of Puzzling Artifacts* (Glen Arm, Maryland: The Sourcebook Project, 1978), pp. 661-62.
- f) Frank Calvert, "On the Probable Exitence of Man During the Miocene Period," *Anthropological Institute Journal*, Vol. 3, 1873, as cited by William R. Corliss in *Ancient Man, A Handbook of Puzzling Artifacts* (Glen Arm, Maryland: The Sourcebook Project, 1978), pp. 661-62.
64. a) Melvin A. Cook, "William J. Meister Discovery of Human Footprints with Trilobites in a Cambrian Formation of Western Utah," in *Why Not Creation?*, edited by Walter E. Lammerts (New Jersey: Presbyterian and Reformed Publishing Co., 1970), pp. 185-93.
- b) "Geology and Ethnology Disagree About Rock Prints," *Science News Letter*, 10 December 1938, p. 372.
- c) Henry R. Schoolcraft and Thomas H. Benton, "Remarks on the Prints of Human Feet, Observed in the Secondary Limestone of the Mississippi Valley," *American Journal of Arts and Sciences*, Vol. 5, 1822, pp. 223-31.
- d) "Human-Like Tracks in Stone are Riddle to Scientists," *Science News Letter*, 29 October 1938, pp. 278-79.
65. a) Henry M. Norris, *King of Creation* (San Diego: Creation Life Publishers, 1980), pp. 152-53.
66. a) "What Happened to the Earth's Helium?", *New Scientist*, Vol. 420, 3 December 1964, pp. 631-32.

b) Melvin A. Cook, *Prehistory and Earth Models* (London: Max Parrish, 1966), pp. 10-14.
67. a) Robert V. Gentry, et al., "Differential Lead Retention in Zircons: Implications for Nuclear Waste Containment," *Science*, 16 April 1982, pp. 296-98.
   b) Robert V. Gentry, "Letters," *Physics Today*, October 1982, pp. 13-14.
   c) Robert V. Gentry, "Letters," *Physics Today*, April 1983, p. 13.
   d) Robert V. Gentry, personal communication, 24 February 1984.
68. a) Cook, p. 341.
69. a) Stuart E. Nevins, "Evolution: The Ocean Says No!", *Symposium on Creation V* (Grand Rapids: Baker, 1975), pp. 77-83.
70. a) Nevins, pp. 80-81.
   b) George C. Kennedy, "The Origin of Continents, Mountain Ranges, and Ocean Basins," *American Scientist*, 1959, pp. 491-504.
72. a) Fritz Heide, *Meteorites* (Chicago: University of Chicago, 1964), p. 119.
   b) Peter A. Steveson, "Meteoritic Evidence for a Young Earth," *Creation Research Society Quarterly*, Vol. 12, June 1975, pp. 23-25.
   c) "Neither tektites nor meteorites have been found in any of the ancient geologic formations [Mesozoic, Paleozoic, or Proterozoic]."
   Ralph Stair
   "Tektites and the Lost Planet," *The Scientific Monthly*, July 1956, p. 11.
   d) "No meteorites have ever been found in the geologic column."
   W. H. Twenhofel
   Principles of Sedimentation, 2nd edition (New York: McGraw-Hill, 1950), p. 144.
   e) Hans Pettersson, "Cosmic Spherules and Meteoritic Dust," *Scientific American*, Vol. 202, February 1960, pp. 123-29.
73. a) Henry M. Morris, editor, *Scientific Creationism* (San Diego: Creation Life Publishers, 1974), pp. 151-53.
   b) Steveson, pp. 23-25.
   c) Pettersson, p. 132.
74. a) Thomas G. Barnes, *Origin and Destiny of the Earth's Magnetic Field*, 2nd edition (El Cajon, California: Institute for Creation Research, 1983).
75. a) Harold S. Slusher and Thomas P. Gamwell, *The Age of the Earth: A Study of the Cooling of the Earth Under the Influence of Radioactive Heat Sources*, ICR Monograph No. 7 (El Cajon, California: Institute for Creation Research, 1978).
   b) Leonard R. Ingersoll, et al., *Heat Conduction: With Engineering, Geological and Other Applications* (Madison, Wisconsin: University of Wisconsin Press, 1954, Revised Edition), pp. 99-107.
76. a) Walter H. Munk and Gordon J. F. MacDonald, *The Rotation of the Earth* (Cambridge: Cambridge University Press, 1975), p. 198.
   b) Laser beams have recently been bounced off reflectors that astronauts

placed on the moon. The increasing time required for this light to travel between the earth and moon has independently verified the measurements described in (a) above. See: C. F. Yoder, et al., "Tidal Dissipation in the Earth and Moon from Lunar Ranging," *Conference on the Origin of the Moon* (Houston, Texas: Lunar and Planetary Institute, 1984), p. 31.

77. a) Before instruments were sent to the moon, Isaac Asimov made some interesting (but false) predictions. After estimating the great depths of dust that should be on the moon, Asimov dramatically ended his article by stating:
    "I get a picture, therefore, of the first spaceship, picking out a nice level place for landing purposes, coming in slowly downward tailfirst ... and sinking majestically out of sight."
    Isaac Asimov
    "14 Million Tons of Dust Per Year," *Science Digest*, January 1959, p. 36.
   b) Herbert A. Zook, "The State of Meteoritic Material on the Moon," *Proceedings of the Lunar Science Conference* (6th), 1975, pp. 1653-72.
   c) Stuart Ross Taylor, *Lunar Science: A Post-Apollo View* (New York: Pergamon Press, Inc., 1975), p. 92.
   d) If the influx of meteoritic dust on the moon has been at its present rate for the last 4.6 billion years, then the layer of dust should be over 2000 feet thick. If the influx were greater than it is at present, as almost all scientists believe, then the thickness of the dust layer would be even greater. These computations, made by this author, are based on the data contained in the following two references:
      d1) David W. Hughes, "The Changing Micrometeoriod Influx," *Nature*, Vol. 251, 4 October 1974, pp. 379-80.
      d2) Taylor, pp. 84, 92.
78. a) Nicholas M. Short, *Planetary Geology* (Englewood Cliffs, New Jersey: Prentice-Hall, 1975), pp. 175-84.
79. a) R. A. Lyttleton, "The Non-existence of the Oort Cometary Shell," *Astrophysics and Space Science*, Vol. 31, 1974, pp. 385-401.
   b) Thomas D. Nicholson, "Comets, Studied for Many Years, Remain an Enigma to Scientists," *Natural History*, March 1966, pp. 44-47.
   c) Harold Armstrong, "Comets and a Young Solar System," in *Speak to the Earth*, edited by George F. Howe (New Jersey: Presbyterian and Reformed Publishing Co., 1975), pp. 327-30.
   d) Steidl, *The Earth, the Stars, and the Bible*, pp. 58-59.
   e) R. A. Lyttleton, *Mysteries of the Solar System* (Oxford: Clarendon Press, 1968), p. 110.
80. a) H. H. Aumann and C. M. Gillespie, Jr., "The Internal Powers and Effective Temperature of Jupiter and Saturn," *The Astrophysical Journal*, Vol. 157, July 1969, pp. L69-L72.
   b) M. Mitchell Waldrop, "The Puzzle That Is Saturn," *Science*, 18 September 1981, p. 1351.

c) "The Mystery of Venus's Internal Heat," *New Scientist*, 13 November 1980, p. 437.
d) Andrew P. Ingersoll, "Jupiter and Saturn," *Scientific American*, December 1981, p. 92.
e) Steidl, "The Solar System: An Assessment of Recent Evidence—Planets, Comets, and Asteroids," in *Design and Origins in Astronomy*, edited by George Mulfinger (Norcross, Georgia: Creation Research Society, 1983), pp. 87, 91, 100.
f) For an analysis of just how rapidly Jupiter would have cooled to its present temperature if it had been an unreasonably hot 20,000°K when it formed, see Edwin V. Bishop and Wendell C. DeMarcus, "Thermal Histories of Jupiter Models," *Icarus*, Vol. 12, 1970, pp. 317-30.
81. a) Steidl, *The Earth, the Stars, and the Bible*, pp. 60-61.
  b) Harold S. Slusher and Stephen J. Duursma, *The Age of the Solar System: A Study of the Poynting-Robertson Effect and Extinction of Interplanetary Dust* (El Cajon, California: ICR Technical Monograph No. 6, 1978).
82. a) Taylor, p. 90.
83. a) A. B. Severny, V. A. Kotov, and T. T. Tsap, *Nature*, Vol. 259, 15 January 1976, pp. 87-89.
  b) Paul M. Steidl, "Solar Neutrinos and A Young Sun," in *Design and Origins in Astronomy*, edited by George Mulfinger, Jr. (Norcross, Georgia: Creation Research Society Books, 1983), pp. 113-25.
84. a) G. B. Lubkin, "Analyses of Historical Data Suggest Sun Is Shrinking," *Physics Today*, September 1979, pp. 17-19.
  b) David W. Dunham *et al.*, "Observations of a Probable Change in the Solar Radius Between 1715 and 1979," *Science*, Vol. 210, 12 December 1980, pp. 1243-45.
  c) John Gribben and Omar Sattaur, "The Schoolchildren's Eclipse," *Science 84*, April 1984, pp. 51-56.
85. a) Harold S. Slusher, *Age of the Cosmos*, ICR Technical Monograph No. 9 (El Cajon, California: Institute for Creation Research), p. 16.
  b) F. Hoyle and J. V. Narlikar, "On the Nature of Mass," *Nature*, Vol. 233, 3 September 1971, pp. 41-44.
  c) William Kaufmann III, "The Most Feared Astronomer on Earth," *Science Digest*, July 1981, p. 81.
  d) Geoffrey Burbidge, "Redshift Rift," *Science 81*, December 1981, p. 18.
86. a) David Fleischer, "The Galaxy Maker," *Science Digest*, October 1981, Vol. 89, pp. 12ff.
87. a) Gerardus D. Bouw, "Galaxy Clusters and the Mass Anomaly," *Creation Research Society Quarterly*, September 1977, pp. 108-12.
  b) Steidl, *The Earth, the Stars, and the Bible*, pp. 179-85.
  c) Joseph Silk, *The Big Bang* (San Francisco: W. H. Freeman and Co., 1980), pp. 188-91.

d) M. Mitchell Waldrop, "The Large-Scale Structure of the Universe," *Science*, 4 March 1983, p. 1050.

88-96.
   a) Violet M. Cummings, *Noah's Ark: Fact or Fable?* (San Diego: Creation-Science Research Center, 1972).
   b) Tim LaHaye and John D. Morris, *The Ark on Ararat* (San Diego: Creation Life Publishers, 1976).
   c) John Warwick Montgomery, *The Quest for Noah's Ark* (Minneapolis, Minnesota: Bethany Fellowship, Inc., 1972).
   d) John D. Morris, *Adventure on Ararat* (El Cajon, California: Institute for Creation Research, 1973).
   e) Rene Noorbergen, *The Ark File* (California: Pacific Press Publishing, 1974).
   f) Violet M. Cummings, *Has Anybody Really Seen Noah's Ark?* (San Diego: Creation Life Publishers, 1982).
   g) Dave Balsiger and Charles E. Sellier, Jr., *In Search of Noah's Ark* (Los Angeles: Sun Classic Books, 1976).

92. h) Rene Noorbergen, *Secrets of the Lost Races* (Indianapolis: The Bobbs-Merrill Company, 1977), pp. 79-92.

97-112.
   a) Walter T. Brown, Jr., taped lectures, available on request, 5612 N. 20th Place, Phoenix, Arizona 85016.

114. a) Byron C. Nelson, *The Deluge Story in Stone* (Minneapolis, Minnesota: Bethany Fellowship, Inc., 1968), pp. 169-90.

116. a) George F. Howe, "Seed Germination, Sea Water, and Plant Survival in the Great Flood," *Scientific Studies in Special Creation* (New Jersey: Presbyterian and Reformed Publishing Co., 1971), pp. 285-98.

About the Author

Dr. Walter Brown has written and spoken extensively on the subject of origins. He is the director of the Center for Scientific Creation and recently moved with his wife and four children to Phoenix, Arizona. Dr. Brown retired from the Air Force in 1980 as a full colonel, received his B.S. from West Point, M.S. from New Mexico State University, and Ph.D. from Massachusetts Institute of Technology. Some of his assignments during his twenty-one years of military service have been: chief of science and technology studies at the Air War College, associate professor at the United States Air Force Academy, and director of Benet Research, Engineering, and Development Laboratories in Albany, New York.

The "Deans" of All Ark Researchers—
Eryl and Violet Cummings

Thanks for sharing your forty-three years of Ark files, photographs, experiences and allowing the author to benefit from your research. "Dr. and Mrs. C.," you are both very special people. All Ark researchers are in your debt.

Eryl Cummings at his desk in Farmington, New Mexico.

Left to right: Violet Cummings, author's wife Carita, Eryl Cummings.

Special Tribute to an Eminent Archaeologist and Ark Researcher— Dr. Howard Davis

The one man responsible for this author's renewed interest in Ark research and arranging for my participation in an 1984 expedition to Mount Ararat was Dr. Davis. He is the founding president of Artesia Christian College and past president of Midwest Christian College. In August of 1980, Dr. Davis was the archaeologist for the only American expedition granted permission by the Turkish government to climb Mount Ararat in search of evidence of the Ark of Noah. He has made public appearances for religious, civic, and scientific groups across the country. Dr. Davis has appeared on many television programs and has held radio interviews in the United States and Canada.

F.I.B.E.R.

F.I.B.E.R. extends to you a personal invitation to become involved in our membership. The Foundation for International Biblical Exploration and Research is a non-profit organization founded by Dr. Don Shockey in the summer of 1985. Among the goals of this research institute will be the acquisition of a central facility to be located in Albuquerque, New Mexico. Contained within its walls will be a computerized library and reference center, video and slide library, film and publication division concerning archaeological, Biblical, scientific and Western Americana subjects. These research and resource materials will be made available to individuals, schools, universities, seminaries, churches, and civic organizations. A speakers bureau with a broad spectrum of topics is available upon request.

F.I.B.E.R. has been the recipient of two major collections of artifacts and photographs including those items acquired by Ed Davis printed in this book. These and many more will be on public display, free to all, as soon as a permanent facility is obtained.

We need your help to make this a reality. Some of F.I.B.E.R.'s projected expeditions include further documentation of Noah's Ark, the Flood, the ancient ruins of Karada and its epigraphic importance, verification and preservation of the Ten Commandments Stone at Los Lunas, New Mexico, and humanitarian help for the stone-age Tarahumara Indians in Chihuahua, Mexico.

Looking for an adventure of far-reaching proportions? Join our membership. We need your input and participation to share God's Good News and Love to the world.

For further information and membership application, write:

> F.I.B.E.R.
> 2705 Juan Tabo N.E.
> Suite B, #242
> Albuquerque, New Mexico 87112

TEACH Services, Inc.
P U B L I S H I N G

We invite you to view the complete
selection of titles we publish at:
www.TEACHServices.com

We encourage you to write us
with your thoughts about this,
or any other book we publish at:
info@TEACHServices.com

TEACH Services' titles may be purchased in
bulk quantities for educational, fund-raising,
business, or promotional use.
bulksales@TEACHServices.com

Finally, if you are interested in seeing
your own book in print, please contact us at:
publishing@TEACHServices.com

We are happy to review your manuscript at no charge.

www.ingramcontent.com/pod-product-compliance
Lightning Source LLC
Chambersburg PA
CBHW070540170426
43200CB00011B/2485